THE AUTISM
FITNESS HANDBOOK

THE AUTISM
FITNESS HANDBOOK

An Exercise Program to Boost Body Image,
Motor Skills, Posture, and Confidence in Children
and Teens with Autism Spectrum Disorder

DAVID S. GESLAK
Foreword by Stephen M. Shore

Jessica Kingsley *Publishers*
London and Philadelphia

First published in 2015
by Jessica Kingsley Publishers
73 Collier Street
London N1 9BE, UK
and
400 Market Street, Suite 400
Philadelphia, PA 19106, USA

www.jkp.com

Library of Congress Cataloging in Publication Data
Geslak, David S.
  The autism fitness handbook : an exercise program to boost body image, motor skills, posture and confidence in children and teens with autism spectrum disorder / David S. Geslak.
      pages cm
  Includes bibliographical references.
  ISBN 978-1-84905-998-5 (alk. paper)
  1. Autism spectrum disorders in children–Treatment. 2. Exercise. I. Title.
  RC553.A88G48 2014
  616.85'88200835–dc23
                          2014009976

British Library Cataloguing in Publication Data
A CIP catalogue record for this book is available from the British Library

ISBN 978 1 84905 998 5
eISBN 978 0 85700 963 0

Printed and bound in Great Britain

DISCLAIMER

As with any program that requires physical activity, it is advised that individuals consult a physician prior to following the program in this guide.

DEDICATION

Ten years ago I began teaching exercise to my first child on the autism spectrum. I never thought it would have led to where I am today...

I have been blessed to work with all my Champions and their families. Adam, Anthony, Ben, Bill, Brody, Derek, Max, Noel, Rachel, RJ, and Roan, you inspire me each day to become a more educated coach, a stronger leader, and to never give up on my dreams. Thank you for pushing your limits with me, but always know— you are the ones pushing me.

My wife Jessica, you continue to support me seven days a week and through my endless hours of work. While I am focused to help this community, not a minute goes by when I don't think of you. You are the love of my life. I love you.

Mom and Dad, growing up I never understood everything you did to raise me and Danny. After all these years, I think I know but I still have much to learn. Thank you for making me into the man I am today. I love you.

Jay, two years has gone quickly. It seems like only yesterday when you called and said, "I want to help you." Your guidance and support go beyond being a mentor.

You are one of my dearest friends. Thank you for all you have done to help me, my family and for the impact you have had on the Champions and this community.

God, the power of prayer is absolutely amazing. Thank you for that day ten years ago and for showing me the path I should take. While the road is sometimes bumpy, I know you wouldn't have it any other way. Neither would I.

CONTENTS

Foreword by Stephen M. Shore 11

Introduction 13

Part 1: Engage

1   Exercise…The Gateway to Building Fitness, Self-Esteem,
    and Relationships 21

Part 2: Educate

2   The Five Components of Physical Fitness—*Revisited* 31

3   Setting up an Individualized Program 39

4   Creating Individual Visual Exercise Schedules 43

Part 3: Empower

5   Champion Stories 53

Part 4: Exercise

Body Image

1   Body Part Identification 74

2   The Pretzel 76

3   Stability Ball Hug 78

4   Arm 80

5   Foot 82

Posture

6 Calf Stretch 86

7 Hip Extensions 88

8–10 Log Exercises 90

11 Downward Dog 94

12 Frankensteins 96

Motor Coordination

13–15 Ladder Drills 100

16 Ball Catch (Large and Small) 106

17 Crossover March 108

18 Crossover March with Elbows 110

19–21 Letter Jumping 112

Muscular Fitness

22 Dumbbell Chest Press 116

23 Single Arm Dumbbell Row 118

24 Standing Band Row (Two Hands) 120

25–27 Medicine Ball Series 122

Abdominal Strength

28–31 Superman Series 130

32 Push-Up Hold 136

33 Elbows "n" Toes 138

34 Partner Crunch 140

Cardiovascular Fitness

35–42 Running Mechanics 144

43 Treadmill 153

44 Cone Running 156

45 Exercise Bike 158

46 Trampoline 160

REFERENCES 162

FOREWORD

One of the most underrated activities is physical fitness. However, a growing body of literature suggests the far-ranging benefits of physical fitness in terms of emotional and sensory regulation, as well as motor control and even social interaction with others. Through my personal experience of having autism, from my conversations with others on the autism spectrum, and in the course of my research into approaches for educating children with autism, I have seen many examples of where physical activity and fitness have led to great improvement in peoples' lives. Countless times I have both experienced and heard others exclaim how well they have slept after a day of rigorous exercise.

David Geslak's work focuses on abilities, rather than deficits, and makes exercise and physical fitness accessible to all on the autism spectrum by providing practical solutions for *engagement, education, empowerment,* and *exercising*—the four "E"s of exercise and fitness. Systematically providing practical steps in an easy-to-implement manner, these four "E"s serve as a protocol focusing on what the person with autism can do in a way that is understandable to those supporting individuals with autism—and also to those on the autism spectrum with sufficient ability to process the information provided in this book.

As a person with autism I was fortunate to have parents who refuted "professional" recommendations for institutionalization in favor of implementing their own—what we would refer to today as an—intensive home-based early intervention program emphasizing movement, sensory integration, narration, music, and imitation. This involved moving to music as well as swinging, jumping, sliding, and other activities on our swing-set, jungle gym, and other related equipment in our yard.

However, due to the challenges faced in proprioception, coordination, and perception, ball-oriented team sports just did not work at all. I hated gym in school. All the coercion from my parents and others to "get out there and play ball" with my classmates brought nothing but tears and frustration as I would exclaim "I hate sports!" My father's attempts to *educate* me by tossing balls for me to catch resulted in my running away. Rolling grounders were easy but I feared that a pitch coming at me would hit me...so I'd run away.

I did catch a fly ball exactly once in my childhood sporting "career." At summer camp while in the outfield I saw a ball descending from high in the air. Unable to look at it I just stuck out my glove, stared at the trees swaying in the breeze at the end of the field, and was rewarded with a nice "thump" in my glove. In congratulating me for catching my first pop fly ball ever, the counselors reminded me that I "really needed to keep my eye on the ball." These examples demonstrate attempts to *educate* me in sporting activities. However, suggestions and techniques from the *empower* section of the book would have helped.

However, I had interests in yoga, bicycle riding and rock climbing. I would sooner ride my bicycle 140 miles or climb a vertical rock face with ropes then engage in games such as soccer, speedball, or bombardment. This type of physical fitness worked! As so eloquently promoted in this book it is important to focus on what does work and then teach what may be challenging through the best way the person with autism knows how to learn. Fortunately we already have those techniques—visual schedules, Power Cards, Social Stories, other social narratives, modeling, etc. It took someone like David Geslak to put it all together.

In combining proven techniques and practice for educating children with autism with instruction and direction for teaching movement and sports, the autism community has been gifted with a vital resource enabling people both on and off the autism spectrum to achieve high levels of physical fitness.

Stephen M. Shore, Ed.D.
Clinical Assistant Professor at Adelphi University in Special Education
Internationally known author, consultant, and presenter on
issues related to persons on the autism spectrum

INTRODUCTION

Physical inactivity is a condition that can be improved. However, this may be one of the most challenging things to do because it requires us physically to move. It can't be done at a computer or by wearing a pedometer on your hip, a bracelet on your wrist, or a device in your shoe. There is not a magic pill, nor will there ever be one. Exercise is a must for all of us. It gives us energy, calms us, helps us sleep, regulates us, enlightens us, and strengthens us—but the majority of us do but not do it.

A study published in *Childhood Obesity* (Egan *et al.* 2013) states that more than 30 percent of children with autism are overweight or obese, significantly higher than the 12–24 percent in the general population of children. I am not surprised that parents are looking for autism exercise programs. For the autism population there are positive research studies showing the benefits of exercise:

> *Children with autism may experience increases in attention span, on-task behavior and [it's] shown to be effective in controlling many types of inappropriate behaviors associated with autism following aerobic activity.* (O'Connor, French and Henderson 2000)

> *For children with autism, a relationship exists between motor skill development, language development, social interactions and academic performance.* (McCleery, Eliott, Sampanis and Stefanidon 2013)

> *Specifically, the use of aerobic exercise with students in various special populations has been shown to reduce unproductive, aggressive, stereotypical, self-injurious and disruptive behavior, as well as purposeless wandering.* (O'Conner *et al.* 2000)

But, clearly, more research still needs to be done.

Those studies which saw the greatest degree of change immediately following the exercise found that within two weeks, maladaptive behaviors returned to the original levels for adults with developmental disabilities (Rosenthal-Malek and Mitchell 1997).

As a parent, you can't afford to and shouldn't wait for every new research study. Your children need to move to fulfill their need for sensory integration, to maintain a healthy weight and lifestyle, and to have another opportunity to connect with you, their sibling, or any significant person in their life. Exercise has the power to go beyond fitness.

As a professional, whatever your field (speech language therapy, occupational therapy, behavioral therapy, etc.), if you recognize an inactivity issue in one of your students you should help to address it in any way you can. Begin by educating the parents on the value of exercise and continue to share this with the other professionals in your student's life.

I have created this book, to give you information, guidance, structure, and visual supports, so that you feel comfortable starting an exercise program. You can begin working with your child or student using this baseline information and you won't have to wait around for someone else to address the potential problem of their inactivity.

If you are the parent of a younger child who is diagnosed with autism, understand that one day your child may well graduate from occupational therapy (OT) and/or physical therapy (PT). While this is a goal you and your child should look to achieve, their need for sensory integration will always be part of their life. They will need a method to calm themselves in stressful moments and a way to continue to improve the physical quality of their life. Exercise is the answer.

It may be hard to understand this now. I receive phone calls daily from parents of teenagers and adults who are no longer receiving OT/PT, and who are gaining weight by sitting on the couch with their iPad, video game controller or DVD remote. Introduce your child to exercise as early as you can and it will make the transition easier as they grow older.

One of the primary reasons most people, and especially children with autism, do not exercise is because the education about exercise is poor. It is often advertised as men not wearing shirts and women dressed in bikinis and sports bras. Yes, while their muscles and abs may deem these people fit, not everyone's body is meant to look like that.

And while exercise has been proven to benefit children with autism, running an exercise class (as part of a physical education lesson, in a park district, or a YMCA) can be challenging at best and organized chaos at worst. Think about this scenario: foreign objects (balls) being thrown and kicked in their direction, bright lights in a room, echoing sounds, and sometimes over 30 kids to a classroom with only one or two teachers...wow! No wonder our children cannot engage in physical education. They must have an exercise environment adapted to their needs.

In addition, it is important to recognize the sensory feelings that exercise can bring—increased heart rate, sweat coming out of the pores or dripping from the forehead, and the feeling of being stretched. These can cause our children anxiety and create physical responses across their bodies that we may never understand.

Do you remember the "Sit and Reach Test," where you sat down, extended your legs straight and the goal was to reach your toes or, even better, reach past them? Well, in the "bible" of physical therapy, *Muscles: Testing and Function* (Kendall, McCreary and Provance 1993), the following was stated about the "Sit and Reach Test":

> *The inability to touch the toes—much less reach beyond them—at certain ages is normal for many youths between the ages of 10 and 14. Individuals with this imbalance may "pass" the test, while many children with normal flexibility for their age will "fail." It would be more accurate to say that the test has failed the children than that the children have failed the test.*

Sad. And guess what? 21 years later, this test is still administered in the majority of physical education classrooms.

If our children are comparing themselves to these unrealistic, so-called "normal" body types, and being put in scary and uncomfortable environments, and we continue to assess them with exercises that simply tell us inaccurate information about their fitness levels, we should not be amazed at the lack of physical activity in America.

While this book provides over 40 exercises, my hope is that you don't skip ahead and begin to try to perform the exercises with your child. I want you to be educated on the structure, the motivators, and the use of visuals, so you will have the greatest chance of success with your children or students.

Throughout the book, I refer to the individual with autism as "the child"; however, this could equally be substituted with student, youth, or adult. The exercises, activities, and protocols in the book have been used with both children and adults with ages ranging from 3 to 60 years. Please note that the exercises will benefit children and adults, of all abilities.

This book is broken down into four sections which will help you gain a better understanding of exercise and enable your children or students to make the exercise connection:

1. Engage

2. Educate

3. Empower

4. Exercise.

Engage

This section is based on my ten years' experience of working privately in schools and organizations with children and adults with autism and other cognitive disabilities.

Often you have to find out-of-the-box ideas to engage your child or student in exercise and any new activities. While some professionals may look at the children as "clients," "case studies," and "autistic children," you must remember that they are children first.

If you are a parent or teacher working with an adult, exercise can be very difficult for them because their body may never have engaged in such a feat. You may have to revert to the same structure, supports, motivation, and patience you would use with a child in order for them to be engaged.

Educate

Once you have captured your child or student's attention, it is time to begin educating them about *why* they are exercising. I will share with you the Five Components of Physical Fitness for Children with Autism Spectrum Disorders© and how they meet our population's needs.

Throughout your workouts, or attempts to work out, share with them the importance of:

1. body image

2. posture

3. muscular fitness

4. motor coordination

5. cardiovascular fitness.

You will also learn of an additional and critical area to concentrate on: abdominal strength.

Even if the child you are working with is non-verbal, they will be well aware of what is going on around them. Add exercise to their vocabulary, making it not only a part of their life but also their language. Their brains want to learn, so give them the fuel they desire.

Empower

This section is by far my favorite. It gives me the opportunity to share my tried-and-true stories of the challenges and successes of the many individuals—Exercise Connection Champions—with whom I have worked.

I have listened to many families talk about their children, describing what they want for them and how they envision exercise to be a part of their life. Sometimes their children were saying, "I don't want to exercise," or they were bouncing from couch to chair, stimming on an iPad, or couldn't say anything at all.

Many times I was unsure if I would be able to engage and motivate them, but I was not going let my uncertainty stop me. I love challenges. And now for our Champions, exercise is a part of their lives and the lives of their families.

Each child has unique strengths and needs, but whatever their challenges are, they can achieve an active lifestyle. Enjoy this section.

Exercise

Here is what you came for. This is your chance to put everything you learned in the first three sections of the book into practice and have the confidence to exercise with your children or students. The exercises follow the Five Components, including abdominal strength, providing you with a visual support for each one.

Each exercise will be described under the headings Objective, How to, How many, and Coaching tips, and some will include a "bright idea" or interesting fact about the exercise:

Objective: This will describe the purpose of the exercise and what you might hope to accomplish. This goal may take days, weeks, months, or years, depending on the ability of the child.

How to: This will provide a step-by-step approach to starting and ending the exercise.

How many: This will describe how many sets and repetitions should be done for each exercise. It is only a guideline: you will have to adapt the exercise to the ability of the child. But remember, less is more!

Coaching tips: This will give you visual, verbal, sensory, or tactile tips that will help you teach the exercise.

 The light bulb or "bright idea" may give an alternative to the exercise or explain why it is important.

Most importantly, try all of the exercises for yourself. If you cannot do them, don't expect your child or the children you work with to be able to do them.

This book is designed to provide you, your family, or organization with a successful start; it is only a map. Each individual is unique, and what works one day may not work the next day. A child may not like sports or a certain activity. Don't force them to participate. Move on to one of their strengths, keep them engaged, and use your creativity as a mom, dad, big brother/sister, therapist, or educator to make all activities a part of their program.

If your organization provides paraprofessionals for the children, make sure they read this handbook as it is not only important to have the parents' support and understanding of their child's exercise program, but theirs as well. Share this book and its strategies with your children's therapists, support workers, teachers, grandparents and others. They may be the ones who can help the children on their journey toward a physically active lifestyle.

Behind every great artist is a teacher. Behind every great doctor is a mentor. And behind every athlete is a coach.

Now go and be the teacher, mentor, and coach your children need.

PART **1**

ENGAGE

EXERCISE...THE GATEWAY TO BUILDING FITNESS, SELF-ESTEEM, AND RELATIONSHIPS

Engaging our children in exercise or any new routine can be extremely difficult, especially if they are older and entrenched in their routine. However, it doesn't have to be—if you use their motivators, and their current interests, that can be the start you and they need. "Easier said than done," may be what you are thinking.

For professionals, establishing a relationship and building trust are vital to any successful partnership or program. However, this is often lost in a therapeutic setting, with an emphasis put on data tracking and pluses (+) and minuses (−). When working in this community it is imperative to remember that they are children with autism, not autistic children. Put the child first and the disability second and it can change your perception and transform your teaching.

Parents—while I have spent countless hours in your homes, talking with you at conferences and listening to your concerns in the community and your needs and wants at individualized education plan (IEP) meetings, I would never claim to put myself in your shoes. I can and will continue to do everything possible with your children and to build resources to help them make exercise a part of their life. And so should any professional working with them.

A study conducted by Dr. Gerald Mahoney of Case Western Reserve University states that, "The facilitators (parent, other) having a visible effect of acceptance, enjoyment, expressiveness and warmth...are significantly related to increase in the child's language, social competence, joint attention and self-regulation" (Mahoney and Perales 2005). This is one of the most powerful studies I have read in relation to autism.

Paraprofessionals—I was in your shoes and have experienced the bites, hair pulls, smacks, fingernail pinches, and diaper changes. There were many times where I had to deal with it and keep smiling. The children cannot always control their actions, don't know what's causing them, and sometimes cannot speak. But it is important to recognize they are trying to communicate with us, potentially *saying*, "The lights are too bright," "I'm hungry," "It's too loud," "My stomach hurts," or even "I'm happy."

Teachers—being a paraprofessional was the best thing for me because it led me to running a successful exercise program. When parapos spend entire days, weeks, and sometimes years with a student, they get to know them nearly as well as a family member would. During my role as fitness coordinator at a school for children with autism, the success of my exercise program was due to the parapros. We were dependent on each other, but most importantly the students were reliant on them. I would give my parapros breaks if they needed it but only if, as a team, we could handle it. So if you see a parapro who needs a breather, give it to them—three to five minutes can make all the difference for your students and your classroom.

Parents—I am sure you have often heard some of the following quotes and can fill in the missing words:

"She won't be able to . . . ."

"He will never . . . ."

If you have a professional telling you anything like this, imagine how they are motivating and engaging your child. Trust your gut and find someone else.

I am here to tell you (and you can help me fill in the blanks):

"He can . . . ."

"She will be able to . . . ."

Professionals, these families too often hear something negative, or that something is wrong with their child. Why add to it? I guarantee you can find something positive to say at the start of your conversation with parents when you call them after school or when they pick up their child from your session.

Instead of, "He is still unable to cross the midline of his body with his hands," it is better to begin the conversation with, "He continues to improve using dumbbells. However, he is struggling with crossing midline but I am confident he can do it. He works so hard."

However, it is important to remember, as a professional or a parent, that you may have to change your expectations of "when" or "how" it will happen.

When working with Kevin, who is non-verbal, wore orthotics on his legs, and headphones covering his ears, I tried to get him to jump his feet together and then apart. I used nearly every visual support and strategy I could think of. After months of trying he was still unable to do it. I would build different exercises into his routine that he could successfully perform, and I tried not to focus on the one thing he couldn't do. Just as I was beginning to lose faith in my own abilities, six months later, he jumped his feet apart and together!

I do not know exactly why it "clicked" that day but it is a day I will never forget. As professionals we have to adapt our routines, lesson plans, expectations, and sometimes our education in order to help our children. We need to think outside the box and, most importantly, to keep the passion we had on the very first day we worked with an individual with autism. In doing so, we must be flexible, and this will not only help to engage the children in exercise, but forever transform their lives.

In order to engage our children in exercise, it is important to understand the elements involved. Staying consistent with procedures and routine is not only vital to many of our children, but significant in building your confidence in teaching exercise.

Here are eight elements that should be practiced daily to help them engage and increase their chances of making exercise part of their daily routine.

1. Structure and routine

When beginning to establish an exercise routine, structure is crucial. Many research studies are done on children with autism to understand what can be done to minimize their maladaptive behaviors and allow them to lead a typical lifestyle. Structure is a critical component to success for our children and should be generalized across multiple settings (e.g. classroom, gym class, speech therapy, occupational therapy, home).

If you attempt to put children with autism into an unstructured environment, you can expect an unstructured response. Even after establishing structure, however, you may encounter maladaptive behaviors from the children when first implementing an exercise program. Keep moving forward and follow the remaining steps!

Maladaptive behaviors in children with autism are often caused by entering a novel environment. Children with autism may not have participated in the services that you or your organization provides. The structure may be something to which they are not accustomed; however, the value it provides is priceless. If parents are uneducated about the importance of providing a structured environment, this is your opportunity to educate them. Continue to change the lives of these children, because even if they can't tell you, they are thankful for your efforts.

I will show you a structure that has been successful with some of my Champions, although that doesn't mean it will work with your child. Even more importantly, you can use a structure that your child already excels with. Don't reinvent the wheel just because it was listed in this book. You then could experience maladaptive behaviors, and exercise may be seen by them as a negative—exactly what you don't want.

2. A picture is worth a thousand words

Some children with autism may not entirely comprehend your verbal instructions. They may understand only a few words in a sentence that you say. For example, if you said, "Johnny, lift your right knee over the hurdle and then your left," the child may have only understood the words "Johnny," or "left," or "Johnny…right…left." You can see how this scenario may become confusing or frustrating for the child.

Visual supports, specifically the Visual Exercise System, or any photo showing a person or character performing the action will help the child to succeed in the program. The use of visuals will not hinder a child's development and understanding of the activity or skill they are being asked to perform. If you are working with a new child or teaching a new concept, visual supports can make a world of difference to how the child performs tasks and behaviors accurately and sufficiently.

I have developed the Visual Exercise System to challenge the children, not the parents or teachers. Available in hardcopy and an iPad version, it breaks down exercises so they can comprehend exercise both visually and cognitively. Ultimately it can lead your children to the opportunity to independently exercise.

If you are working with a child who does not usually need visual supports, then it may not be necessary to use them. However, you should always have visual supports in place and ready if needed. Think of a "to-do" list. If you show the child your expectations, they may be more inclined to finish the activities when these are presented visually and the child can physically cross the tasks off.

Visual supports can include:

- picture schedules

- station cards—describing the activity or exercise

- countdown boards

- first-then boards

- whiteboards

- timers (stopwatch, sand timer).

3. Be their role model

Whether you are teaching an exercise to a child or to a senior citizen, it is helpful to have them watch you as you model the activity or exercise. While a visual support card can be seen as replacing this process, it doesn't. Modeling the activity shows the children that you want to be involved, instead of just pointing to a picture and telling them to do an exercise. That's not fun or motivating. If you can't do or model the exercise yourself, then don't expect your student to do it.

It is also very important to recognize that the children's representation of the exercise will not necessarily look the same as the visual support or your demonstration. That is OK!

When beginning an exercise, if it doesn't look perfect, don't say, "No. Try again," or, "That's wrong, you need to do it right." In the child's mind and body it may be perfect and they may be thinking, "I just did what you asked." They also may be doing something you, as their coach/mentor never thought possible. Why stop that? Encourage, praise, and keep them inspired—unless of course they are in pain or have been put in a position or environment that is potentially dangerous.

Getting their bodies moving is half the battle, and you may have just done that with one exercise! You can always coach and prompt them to take up a more accurate body position.

4. Motivation

Whether you are a parent, a teacher, or a parapro to a child with autism, your positive attitude may be the most important component in any program or therapy. Children can understand whether you are genuine in your actions. They may not be able to process completely what you are saying, but your non-verbal communication tells them more than you realize.

If your role is overseeing the exercise program and the parapros involved, be sure to focus on your staff. If a parapro's non-verbal communication is telling you they need a break or they are frustrated, find a means to give them a break. We are all positive role models for the children and they need our leadership.

5. Patience

Children with autism do not process things the way a neurotypical child does. If you expect that they will, you are setting yourself up for failure. However, just because they learn differently it does not contradict my philosophy of "seeing the children for their capabilities, not their disabilities."

If you provide the structure, supports, and motivation, these children can and will do what you ask. Executing an exercise or activity may not happen in a day, a week, or a month, but one day success will come and when it does, it will be amazing!

6. Use your voice

If your child is not involved in a daily physical education program your voice needs to be heard. Explain the importance of physical activity to your Parent Teacher Organization (PTO) and other families impacted by autism and find out why the school administration does not make exercise a priority.

When I speak to physical education teachers, they clearly know the importance of such programs, but sometimes their hands are tied due to certain state laws and often limited budgets. Employ a team approach when advocating for physical education and make sure it is a part of the child's daily education.

7. The sound of music

Music can be a huge motivator for many children. If it works, use it, even if it means playing the same song for an hour (professionals, make sure you get parental approval). I cannot tell you how many times I have heard the song "A Spoonful of Sugar" from the *Mary Poppins* soundtrack while working with one of my students. Each time I hear that song my smile gets bigger because it reminds me of the way he kept moving his body.

Music is a huge motivator for many neurotypical people when they go to the gym. Look around at all the people wearing iPods the next time you are there.

It shouldn't be any different for our children, and the magic of music can even help them feel comfortable in a gym setting as they grow older.

8. Family is strong

Exercise can provide parents, siblings, grandparents, and guardians with another means of engaging with their child with autism. At home, the family must work together to improve the health of the child in need. This is a team effort and all parties need to put an equal amount of work in.

You may find that you go into the basement for a workout and your child will watch you leave, and then one day your child may *follow* you. I want you to feel comfortable and have a few exercises that you can teach and do with your child. I am confident that this book will help. Be the leader in health and fitness that they need, and, most importantly, enjoy this time with your child.

PART **2**

EDUCATE

THE FIVE COMPONENTS OF PHYSICAL FITNESS—*REVISITED*

Do you remember your grade school math teacher giving you a test and saying, "First to finish gets the best grade"? To some extent, this has been the philosophy behind physical education since the 1960s. The President's Challenge Fitness Test has awarded students for their level of fitness in sit-ups, the shuttle run, the mile run/walk, pull-ups, push-ups, and the sit-and-reach. With these exercises our children are being assessed on quantity of exercise (e.g. how many push-ups they do, how fast they run), not quality (e.g. proper form and body mechanics).

When we work with the developing human body, this antiquated method of physical education does not support a child's physical needs. More importantly, this type of physical education does not meet the needs of a child with autism or any special needs. Each child should be seen as unique, differing in size, shape, and ability. What can be considered notable progress for one child may not represent significant achievement for another. If we teach excesses and numbers we are not educating children about the human body or giving them a reason to enjoy physical activity.

For nearly 50 years, schools have been educating our youth and parents about the five components of fitness: body composition, flexibility, muscular strength, muscular endurance, and cardiovascular endurance. These components have been, and continue to be, the foundation for many exercise programs. While they are still important components for health, the physical literacy is outdated. In the last 30 years our children have become more inactive, more obese (some as young as five being diagnosed with Type 2 diabetes), and there have been more diagnoses of autism and other special needs. And physical education is not a priority in US schools.

When "No Child Left Behind" was introduced in the US, emphasizing better test scores in math, science, and reading, physical education was the first program to get "the boot." The irony is (and I am confident "they" know) that physical activity—the movement of the body, running around, the increased blood flow it provides—is proven to help all of us learn and build new brain cells (Creera *et al.* 2010; Erickson *et al.* 2011).

I have created the Five Components of Physical Fitness for Children with Autism Spectrum Disorders© to combat our children's more sedentary and technology-filled lifestyles, as well as to reflect more accurately what we have learned from extensive research.

The reinvented Five Components are:

1. Body image

2. Posture

3. Motor coordination

4. Muscular fitness

5. Cardiovascular fitness.

An additional component to emphasize when working with your children is abdominal strength. While abdominal exercises could be categorized under "Posture" and/or "Muscular fitness," this is an area of the body that is consistently weak in these children and warrants its own identity.

It is time to give our children, their parents, and the professionals who work with them the physical literacy needed to make exercise a priority.

Here is the definition of each component and why they are imperative to our children's exercise program.

1. Body image
An individual's concept of their body and its parts.

While typically I wouldn't give weight to one component over the other, this may truly be the most important. Too often I have seen, when working with adults, that they cannot identify the parts of their body, and don't know the difference between their right and their left. This is unacceptable.

If we are going to teach our children exercise and sports that involve every part of their body, they should not only be able to identify its parts but also be physically and cognitively educated about how they move and function.

Within this component there are two focuses: body awareness and body composition. Body composition is defined as the percentage of fat, muscle, and bone in the body, and is usually expressed as a ratio of lean mass to fatty mass. Lean mass includes muscle, bone, skin, internal organs, and body water.

Fatty mass is mostly composed of body fat (subcutaneous fat), as well as internal essential fat that surrounds the organs. Body composition will typically be displayed as either a percentage of fat (body fat percentage or percentage fat) or as a percentage of lean body mass (LBM).

Body awareness, or proprioception, is the internal sense that recognizes where your body parts are without having to look at them. As mentioned above, this is vital for beginning an exercise program with your children. If they do not understand where their feet are, or the difference between the left hand and right hand, it can be difficult to teach them any type of exercise, sport, or activity.

Body composition testing (measuring weight and body fat percentage) is slowly leaving our school system due to its negative association with being perceived as overweight or obese. But if we ignore body composition, how will we educate children and their parents about what is a healthy body weight or body fat percentage?

There is a right way to test for body composition and it should be tested to not only educate the children but also the parents.

2. Posture

Any position in which the body resides.

Traditionally when people try to demonstrate posture or "good" posture, they automatically assume an upright position in a chair or while standing, put their shoulders back, suck their stomach in, and stand tall. While these positions or postures help with better musculoskeletal alignment and internal function, they should not define posture.

Our children's bodies move constantly throughout the day, sometimes intentionally and many times unconsciously. No matter what the purpose, posture plays a part in helping to improve our children's health.

Standing and reaching to get something from a cabinet is a posture. Squatting down to pick up a chair is a posture. Within all of these postures your body is demonstrating balance and static and dynamic flexibility.

Balance is the ability to assume and maintain any body position against the force of gravity. Maintenance of balance results from the interaction of the muscles as they work to keep the body on its base. The term "balance" in physical activity is often thought of as "standing on one leg." While this is one form of literal balance of the body, true balance is more complex. Are your child's arms the same size? Can the left leg kick just like the right leg can? Each body part should and can be relative in size and function, even if your child has special needs. And by challenging the body to be in balance, you will also challenge both hemispheres of their brain and also help to bring balance to it.

Flexibility is traditionally demonstrated by sitting down, spreading your legs and joints when a body segment is passively moved and held in position. This is no doubt important and should still be a part of your child's routine, but begin by adding dynamic flexibility in its most simplistic definition—moving and stretching. Dynamic flexibility is an important ability underlying many gross motor skills.

3. Motor coordination

The ability to use the senses, such as sight and hearing, together with body parts, in performing motor tasks smoothly and accurately.

Did you know that a child who can skip can read better than a child who cannot? Skipping, like reading, requires both hemispheres of the brain to work together. The left hemisphere is active when you use the right side of the body and the right hemisphere is active when the left side of the body is being used. The inability to skip is an indicator that both hemispheres are not working in harmony as they should.

When you think of motor coordination, I want you to envision large gross motor movements, such as skipping, running, and walking. But also be aware of the motor coordination and planning necessary to carry out those movements—eye–foot and eye–hand coordination.

There are many activities provided in this book that can help to improve gross motor coordination, and these should be practiced daily. Fine-motor coordination is also important for our children and can be categorized in "Motor coordination"; however, I leave this specialty up to the occupational therapists. I would encourage you to add fine motor activities to your large gross motor activities if your child needs it.

Motor coordination is an essential part of a child's development and each day you should strive to include it in your child's program.

4. Muscular fitness

The strength and endurance of the muscles.

Muscular strength is the maximum amount of force that one can generate in an isolated movement of a single muscle group. Lifting heavy weights once or twice maximally facilitates the measurement of muscular strength.

Muscular endurance is the ability of the muscles to apply a submaximal force repeatedly or to sustain a submaximal contraction for a certain period of time. Common muscular endurance exercises are sit-ups, squats, push-ups, chin-ups, or lifting weights 10–15 times in succession.

Within the outdated Five Components, muscular strength and muscular endurance are kept separate in our education of the human body. This separation causes confusion. Women often think that using dumbbells will give them huge muscles so they refrain from using them. This is not the case and, more importantly for them, using weights helps to reduce their risk of osteoporosis, common in women. Men typically only use heavy weights, which can increase their risk of injury, when lighter weights can be just as effective. And when it comes to working with children, parents and professionals are even more lost on what to do.

The common questions I receive regarding muscular fitness are; "Should my child lift weights?" Yes. "How many repetitions should they do?" Depends. "Is doing more reps better than doing less reps?" Traditionally. "Should they use bands instead of dumbbells?" They can use both. Without looking at the exercise part of muscular fitness, try to focus on the benefits dumbbells and resistance bands can provide from an autism perspective. Dumbbells, bands, stability balls, and body-weight activities can fulfill sensory needs for your children. And many parents and schools want their children to do "age-appropriate" activities. Perfect—exercise fits right in. Even with the lack of inactivity prevalent in our country, if you go to the gym right now I guarantee you will find individuals of all ages exercising.

Muscular fitness is a vital part of a child's daily lifestyle and should be taught with correct form and mechanics. Being muscularly fit can help to improve sensory integration and proprioception. If you (or any instructor) are unclear about the amount of weight to use in an activity, always choose the least amount. If there is confusion about how to perform a certain exercise or how to use a piece of equipment, then don't do it until the answers are clear.

Combining the old components of muscular strength and muscular endurance will help to improve you and your child's understanding of the importance of muscular fitness.

5. Cardiovascular fitness

The ability of the heart, lungs, and vascular system to deliver oxygen to the working muscles so that prolonged physical work can be maintained.

Cardiovascular fitness is often seen as one of the most important components of a fitness program. The heart is what keeps us moving; it must be strong and powerful.

For our children, cardiovascular activity can be one of the most challenging components of an exercise program. When you think of cardio, what do you envision—walking on the treadmill, running, or maybe riding an exercise bike? These are all great examples.

However, just getting some children to stand and walk is an accomplishment. Do not force a child to run if they are not ready. If the child is used to sitting on the computer or playing video games, moderate walking can initially provide an improvement in cardiovascular fitness. Your challenge as a parent or instructor will then be to find the motivators to challenge the child to move more.

If you have access to a pool, remember that along with improving the cardiovascular system, swimming also helps to calm a child's sensory system. Even a small amount of movement has cardiovascular benefits, and over time you can turn this into a large amount.

* Abdominal strength

The balanced development of the muscles that stabilize, align, and move the trunk of the body.

As previously mentioned, abdominal strength is a significant area of weakness in our children's bodies. Having strong abdominals will help to improve posture, can improve gross motor coordination, and even provide benefits for digestion and language development.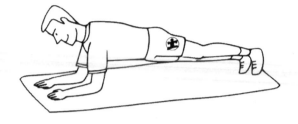

It is important that you see this as a separate component to work on and try to embed some of these exercises in your daily routine. This book will provide you with plenty of exercises that can build your child's midsection and go beyond the dreaded sit-ups that most children hate and typically don't perform correctly.

3

SETTING UP AN INDIVIDUALIZED PROGRAM

Setting up an exercise program can be difficult to do. In fact, there is one question I have been repeatedly hearing for over ten years, "Can you write a workout plan for me?"

My goal is to not make this complicated for you. I want you to engage in physical activity with your children or students and I will teach you exactly how I have done it. The techniques described in this chapter are for an individual session.

I have been teaching exercise to parents and non-exercise professionals for many years and after taking part in my workshops, reading my books, and watching my DVDs, most of them have had great success. You can have the same success with your children or students!

Reality fitness show

Have you ever watched some of those reality weight-loss shows on TV? You will often see the trainer give the participant a goal to achieve, e.g. ten push-ups, and when they reach their goal often the trainer says, "Do ten more!" and then again, "Do ten more!"

Try doing that with a child with autism and you may get a smack in the face. That's probably what some of these TV participants want to do to the trainer!

We all understand why the trainer is doing this to the participant (to help them lose weight and reach their full potential), but for our children this approach will not work. If you give them a goal, once they achieve it, it should be a celebration, a time for them to build their confidence. They should not be brought down because they might not understand that exercising is necessary to maintain health.

Environment

In order for your child to reach the goals that you and your child set, you will have to prepare their workout environment. You will most likely need some or all of the following:

- timers (stopwatch, time-timer, sand timer)
- whiteboards
- picture schedules
- exercise visuals
- sensory toys
- first-then boards
- water and a towel
- lights—with the ability to dim them or turn them on/off
- music.

It is important to have as many supports for your child as possible because in a moment of frustration or over-stimulation, they can help to achieve success in finishing an exercise or routine. Even if your child does not use them in school or on a daily basis, I would highly recommend using supports in an exercise session.

In elementary and middle school, visual supports such as schedules and picture cues have proven effective in reducing transition time, increasing on-task behavior, and in completing self-help activities (such as brushing teeth) in the home (Bryan and Gast 2000; Dettmer et al. 2000; MacDuff, Krantz, and McClannahan 1993).

Exercise will bring a new feeling to their bodies—sweat, heat, increased heart rate, muscle tension, all of which they may never have experienced in this type of environment. More supports are usually better in this case.

Going to the grocery store

It begins with a plan. You make plans or set daily goals. When you get to work you may have a to-do list for the day. Before you go to the grocery store you often make a list of what you need to buy.

When developing a plan to get your child to exercise, don't think about calories, time, and different body parts to focus on—not yet, anyway. Your goal simply needs to be to get your child to participate. Getting your child moving, if only for five minutes, is an achievement! It's a start, and you need continuously to focus on success with your child.

When you make your grocery list, you probably list everything you need in no specific order. However, when you get into the grocery store, I am sure you don't get your apples, then run to the deli section and then go back and get your bananas, right? You get what you need in each section of the store and then move to the next.

A workout plan is similar, but if you are just getting started with your child, don't worry about needing to do arms on Monday and working the chest on Tuesday. That's a bodybuilder's approach to working out, and your child is not a bodybuilder.

The exercises in this book are based around the Five Components of what your child needs, which is constant activity and repetition. You can do the exercises more than once per week, and if you do the same one each day for five days, that's awesome. Your child is still moving their body and challenging their mind.

Sets and reps

Sets and reps (repetitions) are typical "gym lingo" used to describe an exercise or exercise program. Typically these terms are used in traditional strength training (dumbbells) but can also be used to teach any of the exercises within the Five Components. Understanding sets and reps can help you to design an effective exercise program.

Sets: The number of times you perform an exercise, i.e. "Billy will do two sets of push-ups."

Reps (Repetitions): The number of times you perform each exercise, i.e. "Billy will perform each push-up set for six reps."

Three sets of ten reps

Three sets of ten reps are common for what people think is an effective workout for an exercise. This would mean that you would perform an exercise ten times, rest for 30 seconds to a minute, perform the exercise again for ten reps, rest and repeat for a third set of ten reps.

This is not the miracle formula for working out. If you have never done, for example, a hip extension, one set of five reps can be beneficial! The key is setting realistic expectations and goals for your child with autism. It may take weeks, even months, depending on your child's ability, to work up to three sets of ten reps of a certain exercise. And for other exercises it may be quite easy.

Often when working with a child, I begin by doing one set of each exercise. I don't want them to get bored, and especially at the beginning of an exercise program I want to keep their attention.

With one set at a time you can identify what exercises they like and/or excel at. Then, the next time you work out together you can do more sets/reps or find exercises/activities that match their strengths and preferences.

Less is more

Often many people believe the more they do, the better. This is incorrect. People sometimes push their bodies to extremes while exercising. This begins to weaken not only the body, but the mind as well. The proper form of the exercise becomes lost and their muscles, understandably, are weakened. This approach can often lead to injury.

Also, the "no pain, no gain" mentality is not fun and can deter you and/or your child from exercise. Remember, this group of children have heightened sensory systems and may never truly understand the feeling exercise brings to their body. Using a "less is more" philosophy will reduce their risk of injury and prepare their bodies for exercise.

You can vary your child's sets and reps each workout or each week. This variation will not only benefit their muscular and cardiovascular fitness levels, but can also help to improve their social skills and ability to adapt to change.

4

CREATING INDIVIDUAL VISUAL EXERCISE SCHEDULES

As I have mentioned before, visual exercise supports are crucial in your child's exercise program. If your child does not respond well to verbal commands or gets over-stimulated by such a command or by unfamiliar sounds in the environment, visual supports provide a sensitive approach and allow them still to understand the activity/exercise you are asking them to perform.

Visual supports can be implemented with individuals across the age range, beginning in preschool and extending through middle school age. Effective visual supports in early childhood settings include visual schedules to increase task engagement, visual scripts to encourage social interaction, and picture cues to support play skill development (Krantz and McClannahan 1998; Massey and Wheeler 2000; Morrison *et al.* 2002).

I will now provide three examples of how to establish a structure, using a visual approach, within an individual training session. I will begin with the first-then board, then progress to an exercise red/green schedule, and end with a more advanced schedule using a white or dry erase board. I use the dry erase board model often with my Champions. If you have been teaching in the autism community you are most likely to be familiar with a first-then board and a red/green schedule.

Using a first-then board

A first-then board is a visual display showing what will happen after completing a task that is less preferred. For example:

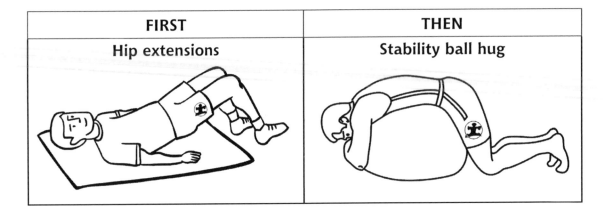

FIRST	THEN
Hip extensions	Stability ball hug

A first-then board is useful in helping children follow directions and learn new tasks, like exercise.

The first-then board can illustrate how you want to get the child involved in exercise. It sets the foundation needed to complete multistep directions and activities and to use more complex systems such as an exercise schedule.

How do I use the first-then board?

Decide what exercise you want the child to complete first (place in the "first" box) and then the preferred item or activity (place in the "then" box) that your child can have or do immediately following the completed "first" exercise. This preferred item should be motivating enough for the child to do the exercise and follow your direction.

It is important to use genuine, engaging verbal instruction while setting the board. If you are engaging and exciting when introducing new tasks, structure, and routines, there is an increased chance that the child will mimic you. Use as few words as possible, "First hip extensions, then lie on the stability ball," is a good example, but be attentive to your tone. Then you can say, "hip extensions are finished, now lie on the stability ball!"

Using a start/finish exercise schedule

An exercise schedule is a visual representation of what is going to happen during a class or within a task or activity.

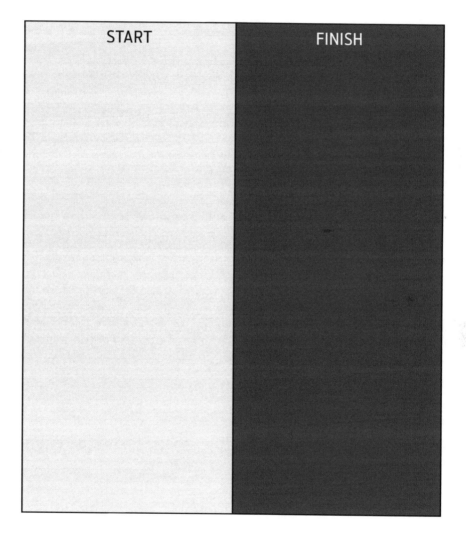

An exercise schedule is helpful for breaking down a task that has multiple steps to ensure the teaching and compliance of those steps. It is also helpful in decreasing anxiety and rigidity surrounding transitions by communicating when certain activities will occur throughout the session, class, or day.

The exercise schedule uses a to-do and finish model, that is usually colored green and red respectively and is commonly used in the special needs community. This red and green model helps the children understand the expectation of what is to be completed.

After your child understands the concept of sequencing activities through the use of a first-then board, you can develop a more complex schedule for a series of exercises during their class or session.

How do I use the exercise schedule?

Begin by choosing exercises that you think your child can accomplish in a particular order. Begin by choosing exercises that you think your child can accomplish in a particular order. If it's possible, try to mix in exercises that your child can do with non-preferred exercises. You can also choose preferred non-exercise or sensory activities, during their transition (time between exercises). For example, use the squeeze machine or draw a picture. This can help make it fun and keep the child engaged with completing their schedule.

Placing small visuals on the left side tells the child that these are the exercises that need to be completed. Review the schedule with the child before you begin. And always be sure to keep the exercise schedule visible to the child throughout the session.

Ideally, you would like your child to carry the exercise schedule with them, but you or the student's aide may have to carry it instead. You could even post the schedule on a wall and after each activity they can walk to it and make any necessary adjustments. And guess what? Those few added steps to reach the schedule are additional exercise for the child.

When it is time for an exercise on the schedule to occur, give the child a brief verbal instruction such as, "Check your schedule."

When they have finished the exercise, you can again say, "Check your schedule," but now have them take the exercise that was completed and move it to the right side of the schedule.

Give genuine praise and positive reinforcements for following the schedule, completing new exercises, and making the transitions throughout the process. It is amazing to see what the children's minds and bodies can do.

Using a countdown board

A visual countdown board is a support that may be used by parents or professionals to signal to the child when an activity/transition will start or finish. The visual countdown includes numbers in a descending order, which are individually removed after a predetermined amount of repetitions.

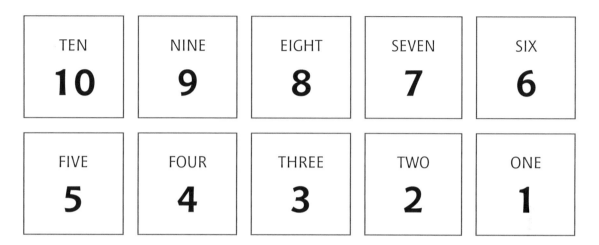

Why might you use a countdown board?

Children with autism may have difficulty in understanding expectations during an exercise session. The use of a visual countdown may help your child to understand the amount of repetitions you are asking them to complete, by visually displaying the numbers during an exercise. For example, you've asked your child to do eight hip extensions, but the verbal instruction may be difficult for them to process, so the countdown board will support your request.

A visual countdown differs from a timer in that the period of time is not precise but can be manipulated depending on the circumstances. If you do not have an actual countdown board you can use a whiteboard in the same way.

How could you use a countdown board?

The countdown board can be used to signal the end of an activity (either preferred or non-preferred) and to signal the sets and repetitions of an exercise or activity. It can also be used in conjunction with a first-then board and a start/finish schedule, for example, "First do eight hip extensions and then lie on the stability ball for ten seconds."

Using a dry erase board

I will now explain how to set up a more advanced visual support system to help children understand the sets and reps they must strive to complete.

Remember, you may not need to use this strategy immediately with your child. If first-then boards and start/finish schedules are effective, then keep using them. I have used the following strategy with many of my Champions of various ages and abilities. Give it a try if you're looking for something new!

In the figure below, the large box represents the dry erase board. The smaller boxes, labelled Set 1, Set 2, etc. are drawn in with a dry erase marker. These small boxes represent the total number of sets that you are asking the child to complete during the workout. To keep the smaller boxes or sets permanent, you can use tape instead of a marker. You can try making an example right now with a sheet of paper.

(SET 1)	(SET 2)
(SET 3)	(SET 4)

Now that was easy, right?

Before each exercise I show the visual exercise support or have it on the ground where we are performing the exercise. As you will see in the next figure, I also show the number of reps to be performed. If the child is verbal, I encourage them to say the number before beginning the exercise. Even if the child has limited verbal abilities I do the same, while also asking them to count with me as we perform the activity. Don't forget to model the exercise and/or do it with your child.

Next, I will give you an example of an exercise, called the Downward Dog, used with Rachel, one of my Champions. The figure below represents three sets to be completed in the four-set approach.

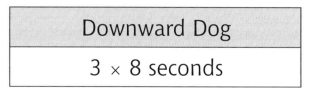

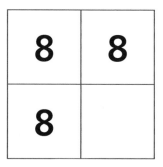

After each repetition you or your child can wipe away the corresponding number, so the child knows it is complete. Once all the numbers are gone the child will know it is done!

Now that we have learned to do one exercise, let's learn how to do a more advanced routine. For this example, I will use one of Ben's exercise routines.

Squat	Standing Band Row	Hurdles—Over
2 × 8	2 × 12	2 × 4

In the figure below I have used different fonts for the numbers to represent the different exercises. Typically, when using a whiteboard I would use different color markers for each exercise.

Still using the four-set approach or boxes, you simply don't write anything in the bottom boxes. All you are asking your child to do is to complete two sets of all the exercises. You may be asking yourself, "Why not split the whiteboard into two instead of four squares?"

I want the child to get used to seeing the four-set approach and slowly incorporate extra sets within the routine when appropriate. Keep it the same from the beginning and it is less confusing for the child.

This approach may not be for all children. I don't use it with all of my children but I have tried it with all of them. For some of my Champions with Asperger syndrome I specifically write out the exercise routine on paper, still including the sets/reps. As long as they see it and check it off after each set, they feel more at ease and are happy to perform the routine.

If there is a visual support system that your child is used to using in a OT setting or in their daily routine to move between activities, don't change it. Use these or any exercise visuals within their preferred system that they are accustomed to.

Changing the structure of the routine could cause a child or adult to become confused, frustrated, and unwilling to participate in exercise. This is exactly what we *do not* want. We want everyone to use exercise as a way to relieve stress, not to create more of it.

PART 3

EMPOWER

5

CHAMPION STORIES

The stories and exercise routines listed in this chapter are based on routines that I have used with Adam, Anthony, Ben, Derek, RJ, Rachel, Bill, and Roan. Each of them continues to teach me something new every time I work with them, and challenges me to be a better coach. I share their background, so you can see how their abilities allowed them to achieve the exercise connection.

It took nearly 12 months to build up to some of these routines with the children, and many of our relationships have lasted years. Even today, for each Champion, each workout can be a challenge to remain motivated. Never give up on the children. They need you more than you know!

ADAM

When I began working with Adam he was eight years old. Adam loves Chicago sport teams, listening to hip hop music, and exercising with his dad. While Adam is limited in his vocabulary and language, he knows his music and sings along as we exercise. It makes me smile every time we work together. Adam is diagnosed with autism.

The first time I met Adam, I also met most of his family, including his mom, dad, sister, grandma, and grandpa. They had many questions about autism and how to help Adam, because, like many families, they were desperately searching for answers and wanted to see Adam reach his full potential. I referred them to additional resources and they all agreed that exercise was something he needed in his life.

Soon after this, we started working together once a week, every Saturday morning. During the week, Dad would work with Adam on many of the exercises I suggested, as well as activities that he knew how to teach. Dad was an athlete in high school and competed in many sports. With the help of the Visual Exercise System and his dad's determination, Adam works out on weight machines, is learning baseball, does wall sits, and works on riding his bike.

The motor planning for riding a bike is very challenging for a child with autism but it can be accomplished. Adam practices on a Spiderman bike with training wheels and, for additional help with motor planning, he practices pedaling on a stationary bike. The task remained challenging for Adam; nevertheless, his father never gave up.

I hadn't seen Adam for about a month. His family was experiencing financial challenges so we had to stop some of our sessions. However, his dad stayed consistent in working with him and using the Visual Exercise System. Not only did he work with him during the week, but kept the same routine on a Saturday morning, when he took Adam to his grandpa's basement where we would normally work out together.

On this particular Saturday morning, before Adam and I headed into the basement to exercise, his dad calmly said to me, "He can ride the bike now. I have been working on it with him for the last two weeks." I was curious and anxious to see Adam pedal the bike. Before our "break" Adam needed full prompting to complete one revolution on the stationary bike.

I asked dad to show me what he had accomplished with Adam. We walked downstairs to the basement and he helped Adam get on the stationary bike. He put Adam's feet in the straps and simply said, "Go!" Adam then consecutively pedaled the bike for three revolutions! I was amazed. Dad and I exchanged a "high five" and I said, "That's incredible, great job!"

Dad's response was something I had never heard him voice before. He said to me, "And 'they' said he would never ride a bike."

Adam is one step closer to riding a bike and he has already proven that "they," the experts, were wrong. Sometimes the doctors and even the highest of professionals don't give you hope. Dads, moms, therapists, and professionals, I hope Adam's story does.

ANTHONY

I began working with Anthony when he was 13 years old; he is now 16. Anthony loves Chinese food—white rice, sesame chicken, and pot stickers to be exact. He also loves comic books. Anthony is diagnosed with pervasive developmental disorder-not otherwise specified (PDD-NOS) and is verbal.

When we first began exercising, I would pick up a comic book and use this as his motivator. During our sessions, he would remind me and say, "You know I'm working for the comic book." "Yes, I know, and you are doing an excellent job exercising and getting stronger," I often replied. I would then remind him that exercise can help his drawing abilities and allow him to be more creative. I did this because not only is it true but he also shared with me that he wanted to be a comic book artist when he was older.

I know he, or many children, may not digest everything that I say, but I wanted him to know how important exercise is for a healthy lifestyle. I have no doubt that Anthony can become a comic book artist or achieve any goal he sets for himself!

Over the last three years Anthony has matured physically and emotionally. He used to stand at my shoulder but now he is almost taller than I am. His strength has improved on all levels of the Five Components and his confidence, much like his height, is through the roof.

Comic book characters still play a role in our weekly exercise sessions but I don't have to spend the money on comics any more, even though I would.

We were working out not long ago and he was performing a Dumbbell Chest Press. His posture was not how I wanted it, so I said to him, "Show me your Superman chest." He first smiled and then rolled his shoulders back and slightly stuck out his chest. I didn't have to say anything else or physically prompt him in any way. Superman did all the work for me.

Just recently Dad came into the basement to see his progress and was thrilled to see the improvements. He continued to motivate by using four simple words, "I'm proud of you."

Three years earlier when Anthony began exercising, his dad, mom, and I continuously encouraged him to exercise independently or with his dad. He would have nothing of it. But just that day, he said to his dad, "We can exercise together."

ANTHONY'S EXERCISE ROUTINES

Routine 1				
Arm Reaches (Dumbbell)	Hip Extensions	Torso Rotations	Elbows "n" Toes	Straight Leg Full Sit-Up
2 × 12 each (2lb dumbbell)	2 × 15	2 × 8 each	2 × 25 sec	2 × 6
Anthony can complete this in just under ten minutes!				

Routine 2		
Assisted Pull-Ups	Elbow Marching	Burpees
3 × 6	3 × 40	3 × 10
Anthony can complete this in eight minutes!		

BEN

When I started with Ben he was 20 years old; now 23, he has always been involved in physical activity. Ben has a burly build and has seen great success in his routines because of his involvement in physical activity from a very young age. During each workout Ben and I listen to some of his favorite music, which ranges from Kidz Bop to The Wiggles, and some oldies but goodies. Ben is diagnosed with autism and is non-verbal. I started working with Ben because his parents wanted to change his routine. The routines and exercises he can do are absolutely amazing and it is a credit to his parents for getting Ben involved in exercise from such a young age.

I consistently use the Visual Exercise System with Ben, which he follows to the letter. During the exercise or routine he often looks over at his exercise schedule and whiteboard so that he knows what the expectations are and when the routine will be finished.

As with many of our children, Ben has a heightened sensitivity to sound. Some days I whisper when I talk to him, and when he is a bit distracted from his exercise, I simply point to the visual and he gets back on task. I don't have to say a thing.

When I began exercising with Ben dumbbells weren't a part of his routine. Because prolonged running was a challenge for Ben, and not the greatest option in the basement, I wanted to find other ways to help him burn calories. For some children, dumbbells can be the answer.

I tried the Dumbbell Chest Press on the ground but he found proper motor planning a challenge, as well as holding 5lb weights in each hand. He had worked on weight machines with Dad at the local YMCA, but dumbbells require coordination, balance, and strength.

Now, three years later, he can do the Dumbbell Chest Press while resting his back on a stability ball, hips fully extended, and 25lb weights in each hand! I embed other exercises in the routine which force him to move up and down from the ground, so not only is he sweating but he is getting a similar calorie burn to that which a treadmill could provide.

Here is an example of Ben's routines and the time it takes him to complete them. These are advanced routines with high numbers of sets per exercise. Ben is a true Champion.

BEN'S EXERCISE ROUTINES

Routine 1			
Hurdles (Over)	Band Row (Double Arm)	Squat	DB Chest Press (on ground)
4 × 3 hurdles	4 × 15	4 × 8	4 × 15 (25lbs each)
Ben can complete this in 15 minutes!			

Routine 2			
Superman's (Full)	DB Row (Knees)	Downward Dog	Crunches
3 × 12 each side	3 × 12 each (15lbs each)	3 × 25 sec hold	3 × 30
Ben can complete this in 12 minutes!			

DEREK

I have worked with Derek since he was 26. He is a bit of a comedian and loves to laugh at his own jokes. Derek loves astronomy, the Chicago Bulls, and to read each night before bed. He also loves candy and soda but over the years has made healthier food choices with the help of his mom, dad, and his many support workers. Derek is diagnosed with Asperger syndrome and is bipolar.

The primary goal when starting to work with Derek was to help him lose weight and increase his muscle tone. A few years before I met him he weighed nearly 300lbs, which was largely down to the medication he was taking. His mother had worked very hard with him to find the necessary medication and to improve his diet. This was not an easy task, but she was able to get him down to 235lbs. Great job, Mom!

He still had weight to lose so we began going to his local YMCA, walking, running, and trying different machines. He had a great fear of many of the machines because he was afraid he would fall off them or get hurt. This is completely understandable, as some of the exercise machines look as if they could be buildings.

After 12 months of a weekly routine with me, and his mom adding a weekly home workout, Derek was able to lose an additional 15lbs. He lost a total of 9 inches throughout his body (chest, waist, hips, arms, and thighs) and now weighed 220lbs.

While some people might have been satisfied with this, Derek continued to conquer more challenges. My favorite Derek story was when we were working out at the YMCA and he had completed his final set on the Dip Machine. It took him months to conquer the fear of just getting on this machine because he felt he would just fall off. This particular day, after his final set, he understood that he was safe and would not get hurt. He then turned to me and said, "I can swim in the deep end." We had been working on this for months, as well, and he was always fearful of the deep end. Without any hesitation, we went to the pool, and after a few warm-up swims, he swam in the deep end!

Derek, now 30, weighs 190lbs. Craving his independence, he decided for a period of six months that he didn't want to exercise but has come to understand how valuable exercise is for his physical and cognitive well-being.

Derek's current passion is watching Rick Steves and Globe Trekker and he keeps a list of places he wants to visit in the world. He volunteers at Dominican

University Library and holds two part-time jobs, one of which is for the Exercise Connection, and I can proudly say he was the first Champion ever hired.

DEREK'S EXERCISE ROUTINES

Routine 1			
Pull-Down Machine (Back)	Dip Machine (Shoulder/Chest)	Squats (Legs)	Dumbbell Curls (Biceps)
3 × 12 (60lbs)	3 × 8 (−110lbs)	3 × 15 (bodyweight)	3 × 12 (15lbs each)
This routine was done in the weight room of a local YMCA. His transitions (time between each exercise) were quick. He would do the Pull-Down Machine, walk to the Dip Machine, then complete the squats, walk over to the dumbbell rack and do the curls. He would do this non-stop, his only "break" being the time in between exercises.			

Routine 2			
Time	Speed	Incline	Total distance (miles)
2:00 min	3.0 mph (walk)	1.0	0.10
4:30 min	3.5 mph (walk)	2.0	0.24
6:00 min	4.2 mph (run)	1.0	0.35
7:30 min	3.5 mph (walk)	1.0	0.44
9:00 min	4.4 mph (run)	1.5	0.54
10:30 min	3.5 mph (walk)	1.0	0.63
12:00 min	4.5 mph (run)	1.5	0.74
3-minute cool down			
Total time = 15:00 min Total distance = 0.88 miles **Total calories burned = 130**			
The Treadmill was one of the first machines Derek wanted to try so it became a part of his routine. When he first stepped onto it, he walked at around 2.0 mph because he was scared. The workout above is advanced and it took him nearly a year to get to this level. Do not rush the workouts, speeds, or inclines. Make sure your children are safe, comfortable and happy when doing a treadmil workout.			

RJ

RJ is 11 years old and I began working with him when he was eight. RJ has a passion for reading, having people tell him about thunderstorms they have been in, and he wants to be an author one day. He is diagnosed with PDD-NOS and is extremely bright for his age. Getting him to exercise was a challenge and some days that can still be the case, but when he does get moving, he works incredibly hard.

My goal has always been simply to keep him moving for the whole 60 minutes in any way possible. His passion for reading allowed me to discover a way to motivate him to exercise. I read and he exercises! He absolutely loves it, and he has turned me into quite the storyteller. He will also read during some of the workouts. For example, RJ will get in the Downward Dog position, I will slip the book under him and he will read a few pages. He will move over or under the hurdles and I will hold the book in front of him as he reads. He works so hard for what he loves!

RJ has come a long way from the first day we worked out. As I have mentioned in earlier chapters, it's vital to establish trust and build a relationship with the children. The first day I worked with RJ, I suggested we went for a walk around his block, which is exactly a third of a mile. I wanted him to move but mainly I wanted to learn a little more about him.

He wasn't eager to do it but I told him, "We will only go for ten minutes and come right back," and this gave him comfort. He then told me to "hold on" and ran to his room.

Mom and I were excited that he had committed and assumed he was going to get his shoes. He came back with a box of Band-Aids.

We asked, "What are those for?" He responded, "In case I fall." Makes sense.

We settled on taking ten Band-Aids. He never fell.

In a few short years, RJ has transformed his abilities. What was once a long, potentially hazardous block to walk has become a secure block that he confidently walks/runs. And yes, without bringing Band-Aids.

Recently, I wanted him to gain a better understanding of goals. He agreed and I gave him the goal of trying to walk/run around the block taking between 5:00 and 5:59 minutes. I wanted him to do it in under six minutes.

He had been working so hard but I wanted to push him even more. He was capable and, while he was averaging 7:30 minutes, I knew he had the ability to complete the block in the set time. Of course, this did come with some incentive, which was a Telepod for one of his iPod games.

I explained to him that it was a goal and if he didn't reach it on the first try it would be OK. We could continue to work at it. However, in about 6:20 minutes, I learned that he wasn't thinking about achieving a goal, he was only targeting the Telepod. When he realized he didn't achieve the five-minute mark he was very upset, nearly in tears. But I think I was more upset. I thought to myself, "Did I just teach him the wrong way to achieve a goal?"

After a few minutes, and a lot of counsel by me, he calmed down. I said, "Let's go inside, do some exercises, and you can try again later *if* you want to."

When we had about ten minutes left in the session I said, "Do you want to try to achieve your goal again?" He agreed, but I was nervous about his possible reaction if he didn't achieve it.

We went back outside, I started my stopwatch as I always did, and we were off! We began with running. I gave him updates on our time when we walked, and about how much distance we had left, "RJ, we are halfway done and it's been about three minutes. We need to move a bit faster if you are going to achieve your goal." At this point, I knew he could hit the target, but he was truly going to have to push himself.

As we took our final turn, I gave him the update on the time and he moved the fastest I have ever seen him move. As he came within 50 feet of the "finish line," he said, "I can do this."

Huffing and puffing we stopped where we began and I read him the time: "5 minutes 45 seconds."

Putting his smile and his sense of accomplishment into words would not do them justice.

These individual exercise sessions have now led RJ to walking home from school, participating in group Zumba classes, increasing his participation in gym class, and having the confidence to swim underwater and jump in the pool. RJ is a Champion!

RJ'S EXERCISE ROUTINES

Routine 1			
Hip Extensions/ Downward Dog	Hip Extensions/ Downward Dog	Hip Extensions/ Downward Dog	Hip Extensions/ Downward Dog
× 8 / × 10 sec	× 15 / × 6 sec	× 6 / × 15 sec	× 12 / × 20 sec
Here he is only doing two exercises but four sets of each. I vary the repetitions of each to make it seem easier for him. He can complete this in six minutes			

Routine 2			
DB Press/Leg Kicks	DB Press/Leg Kicks	DB Press/Leg Kicks	DB Press/Leg Kicks
6lbs × 6 / × 20	6lbs × 12 / × 16	6lbs × 8 / × 10	6lbs × 15 / × 18

RACHEL

Rachel is 17 years old, loves Anime, her dog Fleur, reading, and listening to music. She wants to be an author one day and I am sure she will be able to illustrate her own pictures because she is also an amazing artist. She is diagnosed with Asperger syndrome and before I started exercising with her she stayed active by dancing in her room after school while listening to music. She had never been involved in a structured exercise program and it was challenging to make it part of her routine.

Fleur has been instrumental in engaging Rachel in exercise. Fleur often "exercises" with us and her favorite exercise is the "Fleur" (Downward Dog). However, sometimes she is easily distracted and thinks the dumbbells are bones!

Rachel's transition to exercise was tough. On many days she did not want to exercise, and when she did, she would only wear her school uniform (polo and khakis), and loafers. She would call her mom, sometimes crying, trying to make sense of her day.

I never forced the exercise, gave her time to explain how she was feeling, and slowly we worked the exercises into each session. Her stress was usually triggered by the connections she was trying to make with her peers at school. School can be very tough for any teenager but for a teenager with autism, the issues don't even come close to the "normal" challenges I or anyone else faced in high school.

I would listen to Rachel, share my thoughts, and try my best to help her make sense of high school. I would also educate her about how exercise is proven to reduce stress.

I started her doing exercises on the Foam Roller. This gave her the opportunity to continue to talk about daily struggles while at the same time improving her posture and reducing tension in her neck (where we all hold our stress).

From there, we moved to exercises with the dumbbells and large movement exercises, such as Hip Extensions. There was nothing too challenging, but I wanted her entire body engaged and would ask her to concentrate on the respective groups of muscles she was working, as she continued to explain her day.

Rachel's phone calls to her mom following exercise began to change. She was experiencing new-found hope and optimism because of exercise.

And for the stressful days I am not there, Rachel is able to exercise independently by following her Visual Exercise Schedule. Her stress is reduced through exercise and what were once teardrops of frustration are now splashes of self-esteem and confidence.

After three years of exercise Rachel now chooses to wear fashionable workout attire and her Nikes. She is a Champion!

RACHEL'S EXERCISE ROUTINE

Treadmill	Dumbbell Chest Press	Downward Dog	Hurdles—Over
4 × 4:00 min each	4 × 15 each (10lbs each hand)	4 × 30 sec	4 × 4 each way

It took Rachel nearly a year to gain the ability to complete this routine. She had to develop her cardiovascular endurance for that length on the treadmill, as well as her muscular fitness for the weight of the dumbbells and the duration of the Downward Dog.

Try starting with one set of each for your child and vary the duration, weight, and reps, respectively.

BILL

Bill is 27 years old and a die-hard Cubs fan. He has two part-time jobs, loves video games, and during the spring and summer is the catcher for his softball team. Bill is diagnosed with Asperger syndrome and suffers from seizures.

When Bill was 25 years old I started working with him to help improve his hand–eye coordination for softball. He could hardly catch a ball with or without a glove. I couldn't believe it. With all the therapists, school programs, and sports he had experienced, why was it accepted by his coaches and other professionals that he couldn't catch a ball?

While I had never worked with anyone at this age with this motor weakness, I was determined to have him experience the power of catching a ball. Baseball is the game he loves and he should be able to do what his idols can.

When we started, Bill was very quiet during our sessions. I believe his quietness goes into his determination for everything he wants to accomplish. He is focused, eager to learn, tries new routines, and never backs down from a challenge.

He did tell me, "I want to be able to catch better and be better at softball." Even though I wanted him to catch a ball, I wasn't going to force my goal for him, on him. And neither should any parent or professional.

Typically, when Bill tried to catch a ball, the ball would hit his hands and shortly afterwards (split seconds) I would see him try to grasp it. We began with a squishy, sensory-friendly ball the size of a baseball, and placed it into the palms of each other's hands. When he had it in his hand, I asked him to squeeze it as hard as he could, trying to develop grip strength and get his hands used to the motor planning. We would practice this for both hands.

As he continued to develop, he was able to grasp it the moment the ball was placed in his hand. I then started to back away, tossing the ball underhand to him, trying to reinforce what he just had learned.

We worked on this for months and I started to make it more challenging. With his eyes closed, I placed the ball into the palm of his hands. He was delayed in his reaction time but it improved. I would then put his hand in different positions, still with the eyes closed, mimicking what he might experience when trying to catch a ball during a game. We worked and worked at this while adding other exercises he could accomplish during our sessions.

Imagine working on one thing for an hour that you are unable to accomplish? How motivating is that? Make sure you embed other exercises within your children's workout that can boost their confidence.

Now, three years later, in conjunction with the many Five Component exercises, Bill can not only catch two balls simultaneously, but he can do it while balancing on a stability ball! A miracle? No. Just determination by a coach who saw his capabilities not his disabilities.

BILL'S EXERCISE ROUTINE

Overhead Dumbbell Press	Standing Band Row	Agility Ladder Patterns	Dumbbell Chest Press
3 × 12 (8lb dumbbells each)	3 × 15	6 patterns	3 × 20 (10lb dumbbells each)
This routine was designed by Bill! After we had trained and developed our relationship for six months I began to ask him to pick exercises we had done, without the visuals. I asked him to pick four and perform each one. And he had the confidence to do it! I chose the sets and reps. After it was done I made sure he knew: "You just designed an exercise routine!"			

ROAN

Roan is the youngest person I have ever worked with. I started working with him when he was three-and-a-half years old and he is now six. His grandmother, a lifetime dancer, told Roan's mother that he needed physical activity in his life. That is how I came into contact with Roan and he started his exercise journey.

Roan, diagnosed with autism, has stereotypical autism characteristics, and very limited verbal abilities, but with the help of his parents, biomedical treatments, many therapies, and constant determination, Roan's speech, behaviors, and bowel movements have improved.

In the beginning, working with Roan was difficult. His gut was going through so many struggles, I was new in his life and so was the word "exercise." Visual support played a vital role in trying to get him to focus. For some sessions of 60 minutes, I would have his attention for 20 minutes, in others only for 10.

His parents were concerned and thought that he should be focused for 60 consecutive minutes. I comforted them by reminding them of his young age and that, with or without autism, it is challenging for any young child to stay focused for 60 minutes.

However, after a year of developing our relationship, using visual supports, and putting a structure in place, Roan had many sessions that lasted 60 minutes! I can't and would never take all the credit. It was a team effort, begun with the determination of his parents and followed through with the many professionals working with him in speech therapy, occupational therapy, physiotherapy, and other developmental therapies.

Like most of my Champions, Roan began exercising in his basement. It was comfortable for him. He had plenty of toys and books around, which can become distractions, but I used them to his advantage.

Recently, Roan has challenged me. A boy who was literally bouncing from couch to wall, and had limited communications abilities, could now look me straight in the eyes and tell me, "I don't want to exercise." Honestly, three years ago, I wasn't sure where he would be in his development but he, like many of the Champions, has forced me to be at my best and create new ways to engage him in exercise.

Instead of using the animal books his parents read him to engage him, I now have to use a Storm Trooper mask. Yep, that's right, I wear a Storm Trooper mask that clearly doesn't fit my head. But, in my deep voice, I am able to command Roan to perform exercise to build his strength. And once he completes the amount (written on the whiteboard), he is so strong that he is able to knock over Coach Dave!

Never underestimate the knowledge and strength of your children's minds and bodies. Do you feel empowered?

PART 4

EXERCISE

BODY IMAGE

BODY PART IDENTIFICATION

Objective: To improve knowledge of body parts and basic neural-motor coordination.

– Body part identification can be done in large groups or individually. In a group setting, it is best not to have the children facing each other so they do not model the action of their peers. This will provide you with a true assessment of their abilities.

 As they improve, start to teach them specific muscles or groups of muscles. For example, "Show me your biceps."

How to

– Give the child verbal instructions. If the child is unable to process the instruction, show them the visual support card.

– If they begin to understand then help them to distinguish between the right and left sides of the body, e.g. right hand.

How many

– This should be practiced every day if the child cannot understand body parts.

Coaching tips

– Do not rush your child; give them time to process your request.

– When asking the child to touch the appropriate body part, *do not* model the action. It is important to find out whether the child can verbally or visually understand what you are asking.

– Show excitement at the correct response!

Body part identification

2

THE PRETZEL

Objective: To engage both hemispheres of the brain and while doing so trying to calm and refocus the child.

The Pretzel

 Try this while sitting!

How to

- Begin by having the child extend their arms out, then flip their hands so the backs of the hands are touching with thumbs down. Bring the right or left arm over and interlock the fingers. Next, have the child cross one foot over the other.

How many

- Have the child begin by holding the position for as long as they can, and aim for up to 60 seconds.

Coaching tips

- You may have to help interlock the fingers.
- Modeling this exercise will help.

The Pretzel

3

STABILITY BALL HUG

Objective: Help to relieve stress and calm the nervous system.

 Champion Rachel compares lying on the Stability Ball to lying in a Squeeze Machine. While it may not elicit the exact benefits, it can be a great and cost-effective alternative.

How to

- Have the child kneel on the ground and place the stability ball at their knees. Next have them lay their stomach on the ball and gently hug the ball. Make sure that their feet stay in contact with the ground so they keep their balance.

How many

- Perform one to four sets for 20–60 seconds.

- If your child requires more time, allow it, as long as they are not trying to get out of exercising or their specific activity.

Coaching tips

- This can be paired with other exercises within a program.

- They may want to lie on their back, which is OK, but be aware of their surroundings and ensure that they are safe.

Stability Ball Hug

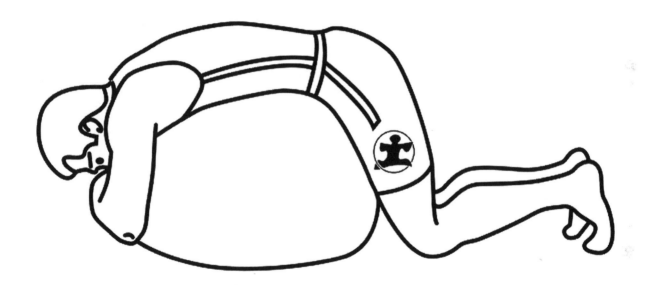

4

ARM

Objective: To identify the arm and understand the difference between right and left and the functions and abilities of their arms.

> Arm Circles are a great exercise to begin educating your child on how the arms work!

How to

- When teaching about the arm or any body part allow the child to take up any position that they are comfortable with (standing, sitting, sitting on a stability ball).

- Begin with verbal instruction and ask them to touch, move, and point to their arm. If this is unsuccessful, then show the visual. If this is still unsuccessful, model what you are asking.

Arm circles

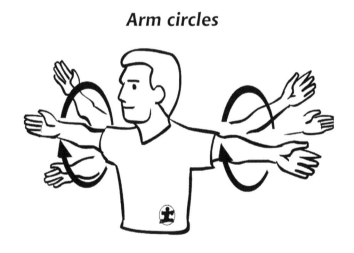

How many

- At least ten times until you get an appropriate response. But if they aren't understanding, do not prolong it. It could get boring, decrease their confidence and cause them to withdraw from exercise.

Arm

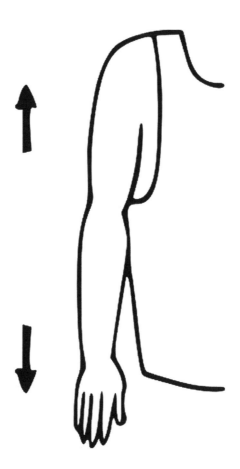

Coaching tips

- Give them time to process your verbal, visual and/or modeling instructions. Remember, their cognitive processing is often delayed.

- Simply asking the child to identify a body part can be boring. Make it fun and relate it to what they enjoy, e.g.:

   "This body part helps you swim when you are in the water. Show me how you swim?"

   "Dad uses this body part when he rows the boat. Which body part moves the paddles?"

5

FOOT

Objective: To identify the feet and understand the difference between right and left and the functions and abilities of their feet.

 Have them kick a soccer ball or football to engage them in using their feet.

How to

- When teaching about the foot or any body part allow the child to take up any position that they are comfortable with (standing, sitting, sitting on a stability ball).

- Begin with verbal instruction and ask them to touch, move, and point to their foot. If this is unsuccessful, then show the visual. If this is still unsuccessful, model what you are asking.

How many

- At least ten times to try to get an appropriate response. But if they aren't understanding, do not prolong it. It could get boring, decrease their confidence, and cause them to withdraw from exercise.

Coaching tips

- Give them time to process your verbal, visual, and/or modeling instructions. Remember, their cognitive processing is often delayed.

- If they have identified their feet you can then try to have them "run fast" or "walk" in place. This can help to increase their cardiovascular fitness.

Foot

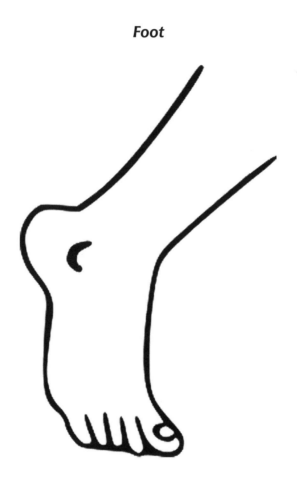

POSTURE

6

CALF STRETCH

Objective: To improve flexibility and relax the muscles of the calves.

 Research has shown that stretching the calf muscles has a link to verbal skills and can help with communication in speech impaired children with autism.

How to

- Have the child step forward with the left leg, keeping the right leg about 12–18 inches behind (length depends on size of the child). Toes should point forward while hands can be placed on hips, the wall, a chair, or a stable object.

- Next, slowly bend the left leg forward while keeping the back heel flat. Repeat on the opposite leg.

How many

- Hold for up to 30 seconds on each leg.

- If the child bounces into the stretch, have them do up to 20 bounces.

Coaching tips

- Keep toes pointing forward.

- Back heel always flat.

- Have the child count while holding the position.

Calf Stretch

7

HIP EXTENSIONS

Objective: To improve the function and development of the gluteal and hamstring muscles.

 Hip Extensions will help to reduce the risk of lower back pain by developing the gluteal (butt) and hamstring muscles.

How to

- Have the child lie on their back with their knees bent, feet flat, and neck relaxed. Then have them lift their butt up so the knee, hip, and shoulder are in a straight line. Control the movement on the way down and repeat.

How many

- Perform two to four sets for 6–15 reps each.

Coaching tips

- Try to not let the butt hit the ground, helping to reduce the risk of injury, while challenging the muscles.

- If the child begins doing this exercise fast, that's OK, they're moving! Each time, work to make it a more controlled movement.

Hip Extensions

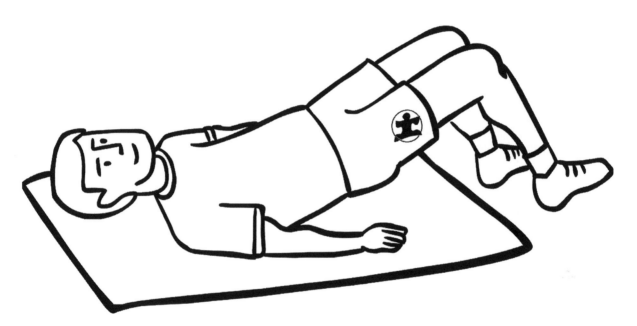

8–10

LOG EXERCISES

Objective: To help improve the individual's proprioception while increasing the flexibility and range of motion of the shoulder girdle.

 These Log Exercises are like self-massages and can help reduce stress and tension in the neck. They are very important for our children but can also benefit mom and dad.

How to

- It is important that you model how to get onto the log. When the child squats down to sit on the log you may have to adjust the log during the process. It is important that the butt is on the far end of the log and that the child then lies back. The back of the head should be on the log and in a neutral position and the neck should be relaxed.

How many

- Begin with 30 seconds for the general stretch. If they want to stay on longer, that's fine as they are in a safe position.

- When performing the arm actions, have them do 8–12 reps.

Coaching tips

- Palms should face up.

- If the hands are not on the ground, that is OK. Don't force them down, as this means that the muscles of the neck and shoulder girdle are tight. This will happen naturally, keep practicing and watch to see the improvement.

- Make sure the neck is not arched back. You may have to prompt to get the neck into the neutral position.

Log Exercise—General Stretch

▦ Claps and Angels in the Snow Coaching Tips

- To maintain stability, make sure the knees are bent, with the feet flat on the ground.

- The arm movements may take some time for child to perform, so try moving one arm at a time before using both arms.

- These exercises can be done every day before and after the workout.

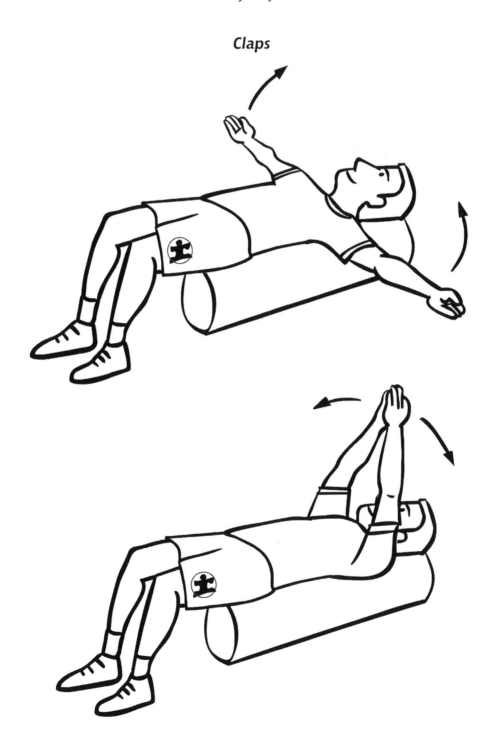

Claps

Angels in the Snow

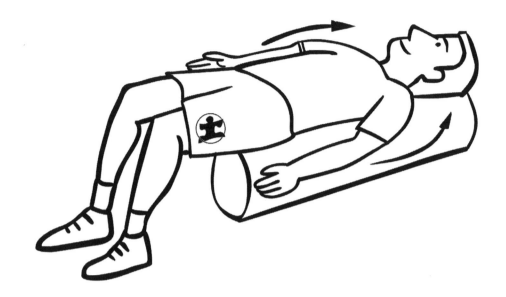

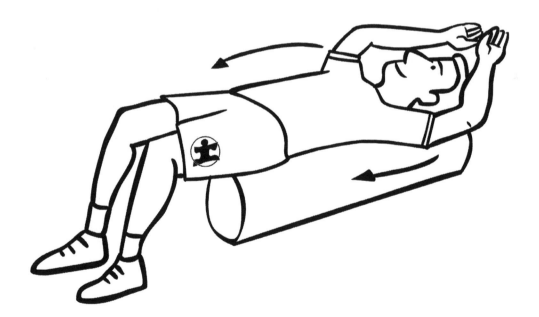

11

DOWNWARD DOG

Objective: To build muscular strength and improve posture and body awareness while stretching the spine and hamstrings.

 Yoga can be a great way to get younger children involved in exercise because they are typically learning about different animals.

How to

- Have the child begin on their hands and knees. Keep the legs about hip width apart and the arms shoulder width apart. Try to have the middle fingers parallel, pointing straight ahead.

- Have the child roll their elbows so that the eye or inner elbow is facing forward. They should inhale and curl their toes under, as if getting ready to stand on their toes, they exhale and straighten their legs, pushing upward with their arms.

- Weight should be evenly distributed between the hands and feet. Ask the child to hold the position for a few breaths, then come down on an exhale. Repeat several times, synchronizing with breathing: up on the exhale and down on the inhale.

How many

- One to four sets of 3–30-second holds.

Coaching tips

- Don't let the shoulders creep up by the ears—try to keep them relaxed, you may have to prompt to get the right position.

- The goal is to lengthen the spine while keeping the legs straight and feet flat on the ground. However, in the beginning it's OK to bend the knees a bit and to keep the heels raised, especially for younger children whose bodies are still growing.

Downward Dog

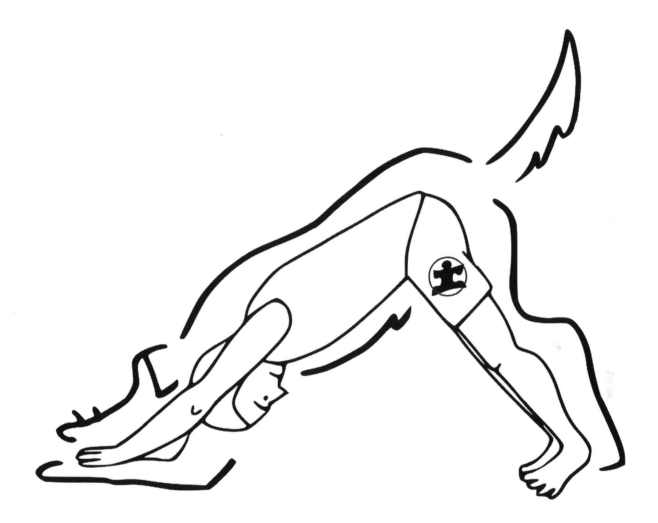

12

FRANKENSTEINS

Objective: To improve dynamic flexibility while crossing the midline of the body.

 Another alternative to teach crossing the midline of the body and further challenging their abilities.

How to

- Have the child begin by standing tall, with good posture, and looking straight ahead. It is important to model the exercise, facing the child.

- Ask them to walk forward, and in doing so touch their right hand to left toe and then left hand to right toe. Model this as well.

- Try to maintain good posture.

How many

- One to four sets of 3–30-second holds.

Coaching tips

- You may have to do a lot of prompting to get them started.

- If their legs do not remain straight, that is OK, especially if they are crossing the midline.

- If they can't do it going forward, try it going backward.

Frankensteins

MOTOR
COORDINATION

13–15

LADDER DRILLS

Objective: To improve foot–eye coordination. Three exercises can be practiced: 2-In Forward, 2-In Lateral, 2-Foot Hops.

 Ladders can be made with masking tape to use indoors or sidewalk chalk to use outdoors.

2-IN FORWARD

How to

- To help the child perform this exercise, modeling should be used. You can place footprints on the ground, as shown in the example. Also show the child a visual support card that describes the exercise.

- When demonstrating, walk through the exercise using big body movements to show the child what you want them to do. You want the child to place each foot into the four squares with the same pattern of movement (i.e. right foot then left foot).

- You are asking the child to perform this exercise in two different ways, leading with the right foot (as in the example) and then leading with the left foot.

How many

- One to four repetitions leading with each leg.

▨ Coaching tips

– Instead of using footprints you can also use colors for them to step on, or pictures of something interesting they may like...or not like.

– If it doesn't look perfect, that's OK! Keep encouraging and practicing. Getting them moving is half the battle.

– When creating the ladder, 12 inches × 12 inches, works best, but for the younger population you may want to create smaller boxes.

Ladder Drills—2-In Forward

2-IN LATERAL

How to

- To help the child complete this exercise, modeling should be used. Place footprints on the ground, as shown in the example. Also show the child a visual support card that describes the exercise.

- When demonstrating, walk through the exercise using big body movements to show the child what you want them to do. You want the child to place each foot into the four squares with the same pattern of movement (i.e. right foot then left foot). The feet should not cross!

- The child should be moving laterally (side-to-side). Have the child face you or use an object/motivator to help put them into the correct position.

- You are asking the child to perform this exercise in two different ways, leading with the left foot (as in the above example) and then leading with the right foot.

 Moving laterally challenges not only the muscles of the ankles, knees, and hips but also the brain!

How many

- One to four repetitions leading with each leg.

Coaching tips

- Holding their hands, facing them, may help them understand that you want them to move side-to-side.

- Tell the child to make up their own pattern, as this will encourage them to take ownership of the exercise.

Ladder Drills—2-In Lateral

2-FOOT HOPS

How to

- To help the child complete this exercise, modeling should be used. You can place footprints on the ground, as shown in the example. Also show the child a visual support card that describes the exercise.

- When demonstrating, jump through the exercise slowly, showing the child what you want them to do. You want the child to jump with feet together into the four squares. Speed is not important. Getting through the pattern is what matters.

- You are asking the child to perform this exercise in two different ways, hopping forward and hopping backward. If the child looks backward when hopping in that direction, that is fine.

 Instead of having them jump on footprints, try using pictures of characters from their favorite movies or even of the evil bad guys!

How many

- One to four repetitions hopping forward and backward.

Coaching tips

- As you ask them to jump forward, face them with your feet in the ladder and jump backward. You may want to hold their hands when doing this.

- Use a count down to get them started, i.e. "Ready...3, 2, 1...go."

- Be patient, the ability to jump is very challenging for our children.

- You can try putting a small box or book for them to jump to and down from.

Ladder Drills—2-Foot Hops

16

BALL CATCH (LARGE AND SMALL)

Objective: To improve eye–hand coordination.

 An overhand toss can be very threatening for a child. Begin with an underhand toss, starting close together.

How to

- The child should stand facing you or their partner approximately 2–4 feet away. Marking an "X" on the ground with masking tape, or using a cone, may help to put the child in position. You should then throw a large ball (basketball, or a ball similar in size) to the child using an underhand toss. The child should attempt to catch the ball using fingers and hands only.

- When using a small ball (baseball or ball similar in size) the set-up procedure is the same as it is for the large ball. However, you can give the child a physical prompt by touching the appropriate hand to catch with, or you can model this or physically prompt the child to put the opposite hand behind their back. The child should attempt to catch the ball using their palm and fingers.

How many

- Perform one to four sets of 5–15 catch attempts.

Coaching tips

- Use a ball that is comfortable for the child—one that is squishy or visually stimulating is very good.

- Practicing throwing and catching with the non-dominant hand can help to improve the motor planning of the dominant hand.

Ball Catch (Large)

Ball Catch (Small)

17

CROSSOVER MARCH

Objective: To cross consecutively the midline of the body using opposite arms and legs while improving motor coordination.

 This is a great exercise for a classroom break because it utilizes both hemispheres of the brain.

How to

- This exercise can help improve the mechanics of walking and running. Make an "X" on the ground or use a cone as a visual marker for the child to stand on. It is best to model this exercise once for the child.

- The goal is for the child to march in place, bringing their right knee up and touching it with their left hand, and then bringing the left knee up and touching it with the right hand.

How many

- Try for six consecutive touches and then go for more. Have the child count while they do it too!

Coaching tips

- You may need to give a physical prompt to get them to touch the appropriate hand to the correct knee. Before a full prompt, try tapping the appropriate leg and knee.

- If they can't perform it standing in one place, have them walk in a circle or walk forward and backward. I have had a lot of success with this approach.

Crossover March

18

CROSSOVER MARCH WITH ELBOWS

Objective: To cross consecutively the midline of the body using opposite arms and elbows while improving motor coordination and building abdominal strength.

 Using the elbows challenges the abdominals.

How to

- Make an "X" on the ground with tape or provide a visual marker for the child to stand on. It is best to model this exercise for the child as well as showing the visual.

- Have the child bring the right knee up and touch it with the left elbow and then bring the left knee up and touch it with the right elbow.

How many

- One to four sets of 6–30 reps.

Coaching tips

- You may need to give a physical prompt to get them to touch the appropriate knee to the correct elbow. Before a full prompt, try tapping the appropriate knee and elbow.

- If the child cannot perform it standing in one place, have them walk in a circle or walk forward and backward. I have seen a lot of success when a child does this in motion.

Crossover March with Elbows

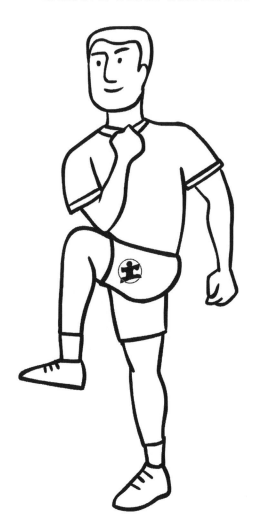

19–21

LETTER JUMPING

Objective: To improve gross motor coordination and strengthen the muscles of the ankles, knees, and hips while increasing the knowledge of letters.

 After they jump the letter, have them write the letter on the whiteboard. Then you have just added a fine motor activity!

How to

- Make five dots on the ground using masking tape, chalk, or spray paint. Arrange the dots 1–2 feet apart similar to the examples above.

- Always have the child start with double leg jumps. Have them starting on the appropriate dot to the letter they are going to "spell." For example, if spelling "M," the child would begin on the bottom left dot. If spelling "X," one foot would be on bottom left, the other on bottom right. They then jump to the middle with both feet and finish the way they started at the top two dots.

How many

- Correctly spell each letter once. When the child has got the hang of it, you can repeat for up to five sets per session.

Coaching tips

- If the child walks instead of jumps to spell the letter, that is great! Their brain is processing the letters in another way. The jumping may take more time.

- If jumping with two feet becomes easy for the child, have them try jumping the letters on one leg. Make sure to do both legs.

Letter Jumping—Double Leg Jumps

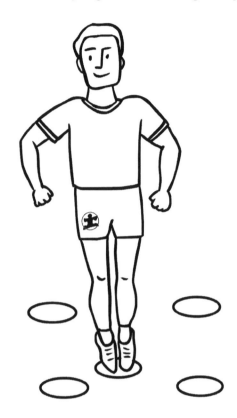

Letter Jumping—Single Leg Jumps

Try jumping these letters

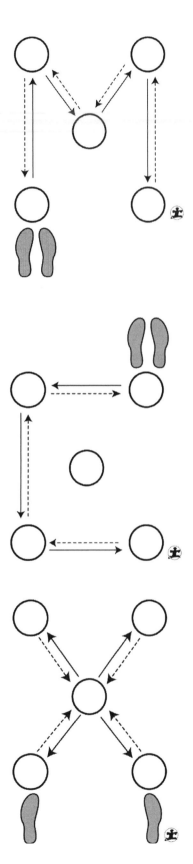

MUSCULAR FITNESS

22

DUMBBELL CHEST PRESS

Objective: To strengthen the muscles of the upper body (pectorals–chest, deltoids—shoulder, triceps—back of arms), while providing sensory feedback.

 You must assist or spot the child during this exercise. Do not assist at the wrists, hold or spot the dumbbells!

How to

- Have the child lie on their back with knees bent, feet flat, and neck relaxed. Then hand the child the dumbbells. Next, hold your hands over the child's chest and have them push the dumbbells toward your hands.

- Then have the child return the dumbbells back to the starting position, tapping the back of their arms on the ground and repeating the exercise.

How many

- One to four sets of 6–20 repetitions.

Coaching tips

- If you have a bench for your child you can use it but it may be more appropriate for a teenager or adult. Lying on the ground may be safer and allow them to control the movement better.

- If a child's feet cannot comfortably reach the floor when lying on a bench, do not use the bench.

Dumbbell Chest Press

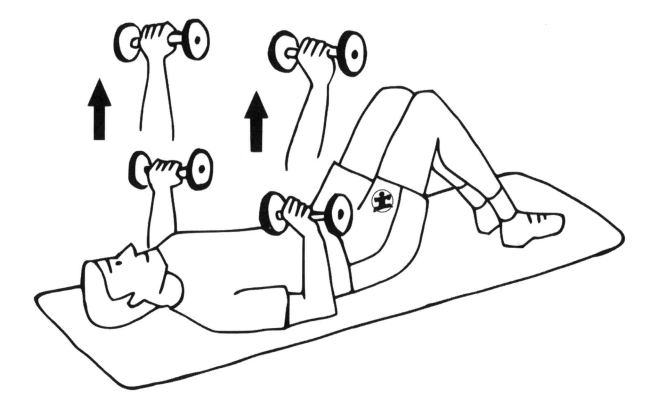

23

SINGLE ARM DUMBBELL ROW

Objective: To improve the muscular fitness of the back and shoulder girdle.

How to

- Have the child begin with their hands and knees on the ground. Make sure the spine is in alignment (straight) and their eyes are looking at the ground.

- Next have the child grab the dumbbell with one hand. Place your hand above the child's elbow. Then have the child lift the weight up until their elbow touches your hand.

- Have the child slowly lower the weight and repeat. Make sure they perform the exercise on both arms.

- Always begin with lighter dumbbells before moving on to heavier ones.

How many

- Four sets of 6–20 reps.

Coaching tips

- In order to get a full range of motion you may need to put your other hand at the starting position (bottom) so the child also touches there.

- If the child alternates repetitions between hands (first right, then left), that is fine. Again, anything to keep their bodies moving as long as they are safe.

Single Arm Dumbbell Row

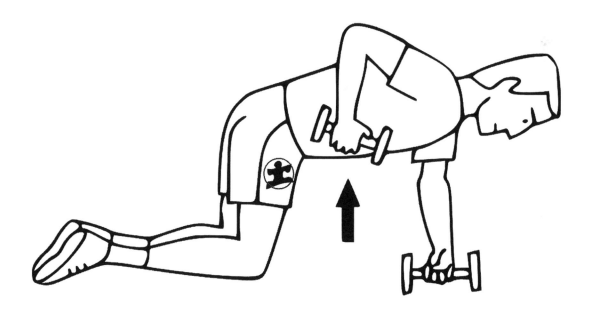

24

STANDING BAND ROW (TWO HANDS)

Objective: To improve posture and the muscular fitness of the back muscles.

 Try doing it with one hand. This is another opportunity for you to teach the difference between right and left.

How to

- Wrap the band around a basement post or anything stable and secure. Next, give the handles to the child and step behind them.

- Then, ask the child to pull the band, prompting their elbows to hit your hands. This will help them understand the range of motion they need to complete.

How many

- 1–4 sets of 6–20 pulls.

Coaching tips

- When the child is pulling the bands toward your hands, look at the middle of their back and if the shoulder blades do not pinch, move your hands further back for the elbows to touch.

Standing Band Row (One Hands)

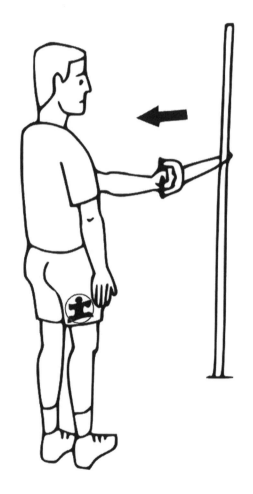

Standing Band Row (Two hand)

25–27

MEDICINE BALL SERIES

Objective: To improve the fitness of the muscles of the chest, shoulders, and arms.

MEDICINE BALL CHOP

How to

– Have the child begin with the medicine ball away from the chest and with the arms straight. Slowly lift the medicine ball over the head keeping the arms straight.

– When bringing the medicine ball down, the child should lower it slowly, keeping the arms straight.

How many

– Perform one to three sets of 3–12 reps.

Coaching tips

– Always begin with a lightweight medicine ball.

– You may need to guide the child's arms into the correct position for the first few repetitions.

Medicine Ball Chop

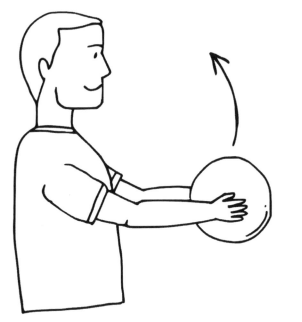

Start

Medicine Ball Chop

Finish

MEDICINE BALL OVERHEAD PRESS

How to

- Have the child begin with the medicine ball at chest level, arms bent, with both hands firmly on the sides of the medicine ball.

- They then push or press the medicine ball over their head with their arms near to full extension.

How many

- Perform one to three sets of 3–12 reps.

Coaching tips

- To help the child reach full extension, have them hit your hand or an object with the ball above the head.

- The knees should have a slight bend and their upper body should be standing tall, not hunched over in any way.

Medicine Ball Overhead Press

Start

Medicine Ball Overhead Chop

Finish

MEDICINE BALL PARTNER PASS

 An advanced exercise is medicine ball chest passes, similar to chest passes with a basketball.

How to

- Have the child begin by firmly gripping the sides of the medicine ball, keeping it level with the chest.

- A partner should be standing in front of them, with their arms about two feet from the medicine ball at chest level.

- Make sure before the medicine ball is passed they are looking at each other and/or the medicine ball. You can also have them say their partner's name before they throw the medicine ball, i.e. "John, catch the ball."

How many

- Perform one to three sets of 3–12 repetitions.

Coaching tips

- If the medicine ball starts dropping through the movement, replace it with a lighter medicine ball.

- You may begin by having them simply hand the medicine ball back and forth.

- Counting backward (e.g. 3...2...1) can better help the child to understand when the activity will be finished.

Medicine Ball Partner Pass

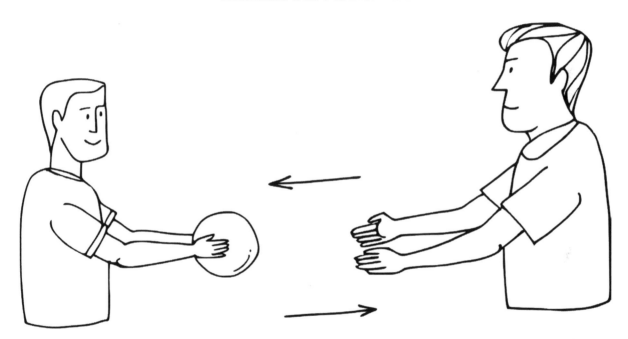

ABDOMINAL STRENGTH

28–31

SUPERMAN SERIES

Objective: To develop abdominal strength, balance, and the range of motion of the shoulders and legs, while working to improve crossing the midline of the body.

The first two exercises in this series are preparation for the full Superman Exercise.

LEG KICKS

Objective: To increase the range of motion in the hips and legs, while challenging the abdominals to perform the full Superman Exercise.

 If the child does not extend their leg, place your hand above the leg to give them something to reach for.

▨ How to

- Have the child begin on their hands and knees, making sure the spine is in alignment and the eyes are looking at the ground.

- Next, have the child extend their right or left leg out. You may have to tap their leg to let them know which leg you want them to use.

- Then, make sure they return to the starting position and repeat. If they rest the knee as they return, that is fine. Your goal should be that they don't rest, and you keep them in constant movement.

▨ How many

- One to four sets each leg of 6–15 reps.

Coaching tips

- This exercise is a perfect opportunity to teach them the difference between right and left.

Superman Series—Leg Kicks

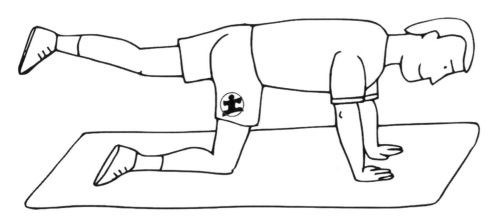

Superman Series—Leg Kicks With Hands

ARM REACHES

Objective: To cross the midline of the body and increase the range of motion of the shoulder girdle while working to perform the Superman Exercise.

 Placing a small dumbbell (1lb) in their hand can help to build more strength in the shoulder girdle.

How to

- Have the child begin on their hands and knees, making sure the spine is in alignment, and their eyes are looking at the ground.

- Next, have the child use the right or left hand and first touch the opposite knee and then reach out or toward your hand.

- Repeat with the opposite hand.

- Emphasize the importance of—and praise—the touching of the opposite knee before the child reaches for your hand.

How many

- One to four sets for each hand of 6–15 reps.

Coaching tips

- If you move your hand to different positions for them to reach, this will work different muscles of the shoulder girdle.

- This exercise should be done in isolation, even if they can perform the full Superman Exercise.

- To help them touch the opposite knee, try sliding their hand on the ground or carpet, which will help because of the sensory perception they will receive.

Arm Reaches

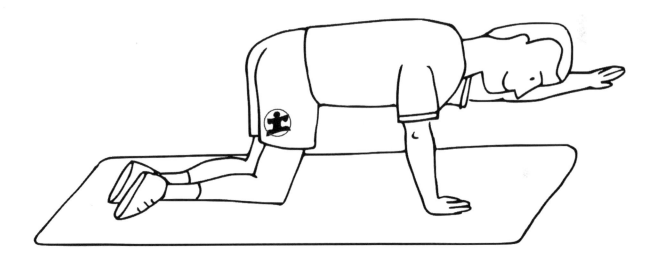

SUPERMAN

Objective: To cross the midline of the body by touching the opposite knee and hand together below the stomach and then fully extend the arm and leg.

 If your child has difficulty with sit-ups or crunches this is a great alternative to build abdominal strength.

How to

- Have the child begin on their hands and knees, making sure the spine is in alignment and their eyes are looking at the ground.

- Next, have the child touch their right hand to the opposite knee (left) and then extend the right hand and left leg, simultaneously. Do one side at a time and then repeat with the left hand and right leg.

- As the child continues the amount of repetitions you give them, ideally you do not want them to rest their working hand/leg at any point. However, this exercise is complex, so if the child needs a break in order to process the information, allow this.

How many

- One to four sets of 6–20 reps each side.

Coaching tips

- This is challenging! If your child does not get it on the first try, don't worry. The key is breaking it down. Follow the visuals and use the exercises earlier in the series to help your child achieve success.

Superman

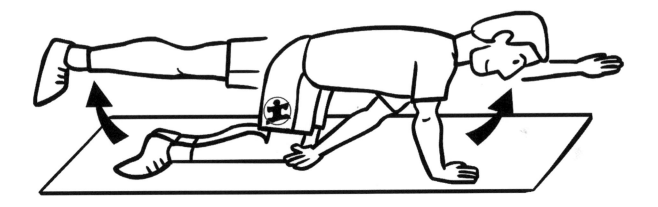

32

PUSH-UP HOLD

Objective: To improve the muscular fitness of the abdominals, arms, glutes/hamstrings, and shoulder girdle.

 They *do not* do a push-up. Just have them try to hold this position.

How to

- Have the child start on the ground on their hands and knees.

- Next, make sure the hands are flat on the ground or mat, with the chest directly over the hands.

- Then, have them put one leg straight back, with the toes or ball of the foot on the ground, then follow with the other leg.

- Be patient, this is a challenging exercise for the entire body.

How many

- One to three sets for 5–20 seconds.

Coaching tips

- You want to imagine a straight line drawn through the shoulder, hip, knee, and ankle.

- At the beginning, you may have to physically prompt to get their hips up and prevent them from sinking.

- Start slowly, holding for between 3 and 8 seconds, and gradually increase the length of time.

Push-Up Hold

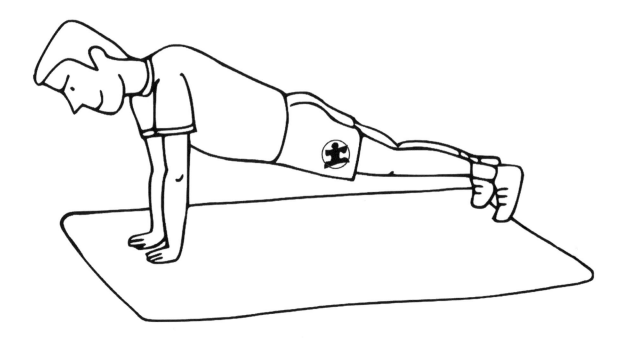

33

ELBOWS "N" TOES

Objective: To strengthen the muscles of the abdominal, glutes, hamstrings, and shoulder girdle.

 This exercise works the entire body and can be more effective and safer than a traditional sit-up or crunch.

How to

- To help the child complete this exercise, you should model it. If necessary, show the child a visual support card that describes the exercise.

- Have the child begin with forearms and palms flat on the floor. Next, have the child place their legs straight back, toes pushing into the floor. You want the child to maintain a flat back (the butt should not be too high or sinking).

How many

- One to four sets for 5–20 seconds.

Coaching tips

- Have the child try holding a push-up position first.

- If the child can perform the exercise, try tapping them on their shoulders, sides of the torso, and legs as they do it. This further challenges the muscles of the abdominals.

- Make sure their neck stays relaxed, eyes looking at the ground.

- If the butt is high in the air, that is OK, but try to get their hips down. Their body may shake at this point but that is OK and just shows that the exercise is effective.

Elbows "n" Toes

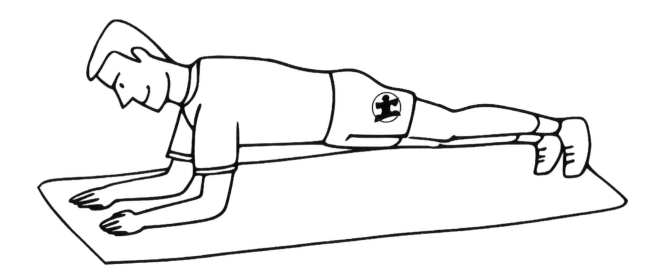

34

PARTNER CRUNCH

Objective: To strengthen the abdominal muscles while working on teamwork.

 A great exercise for building social skills with your children or students.

How to

- Have one child performing the crunch, lying on their back, knees bent, feet flat. Have their partner, or you, stand near their feet with arms extended out.

- Have the child extend their arms out and then crunch up to touch your or their partner's hands. Only their shoulder blades need to come off the ground, not their entire body. If their body is coming up, adjust your or their partner's hand and body position to be closer to them.

How many

- One to four sets for 5–15 reps.

Coaching tips

- Have the children count together while doing the exercises.

- If the child is working with a partner, make sure they switch and learn to do both positions.

Partner Crunch

CARDIOVASCULAR FITNESS

35–42

RUNNING MECHANICS

(Wide Run/Tight Rope, Least Amount/As Many Steps, Quiet Feet/Loud Feet, Fast Arms/No Arms)

Objective: To improve gross motor coordination, which will help the mechanics of running, walking, and large gross motor activities.

This is a series of running forms that ideally should be practiced together. Try doing them in pairs (i.e. first Wide Run, then Tight Rope, etc.). If they cannot be practiced all at once, that is fine. Choose the ones that the child may like and then gradually try the others.

How to

- Pick a distance that is realistic for your child to run/walk and use cones or two objects or lines on the ground that give a start and end point.

- If you have a start and stop visual support card, place it at the appropriate location.

- To have the child begin the exercise it is important to use the same countdown and cadence. For example, "Ready...set...go," "Down...set...hike," or "3...2...1... go!"

- If auditory processing is tough for the child, try using an arm movement to start the exercise. For example, raise your arm up in the air, then drop your arm to signify "start," and the child will go. Be sure to demonstrate this for the child.

- Modeling each of these exercises is important.

How many

- One to ten set(s) of 5–20 yards for each run.

WIDE RUN

Wide Run

Coaching tips

- If it looks funny, that's a good thing.
- Encourage getting the "knees up" as they run.

TIGHT ROPE RUN

Tight Rope Run

Coaching tips

- Footprints on the ground will help (as pictured), as will drawing a line with chalk outside or using masking tape indoors.

- For a more advanced exercise, try doing this on a curb. Use caution: start with walking, jogging, and then running.

LEAST AMOUNT OF STEPS

Least Amount of Steps

Coaching tips

- It should almost look as if they are leaping or reaching to step on something.

- Place visual markers a distance between 3 and 5 feet apart, depending on the child's size and ability.

AS MANY STEPS AS POSSIBLE

As Many Steps As Possible

Coaching tips

- Emphasize getting the "knees up" as they run; sometimes the child may shuffle their feet across the ground.

- Watch what the arms do. Are they moving in opposition? Are they just hanging by the sides? When the child is confident with this exercise, then start to talk about arm action.

LOUD STEPS

Loud Steps

Coaching tips

- You don't want them stomping their way to the finish but making a satisfyingly loud noise with their feet while trying to maintain proper running mechanics.

- If they are hoping or skipping to do it, that's OK.

QUIET FEET

Quiet Feet

Coaching tips

- Tell child to "Be quiet like a cat."
- Have them start by standing on their tiptoes.

FAST ARMS

Fast Arms

 If the child is having trouble, take the legs out of it. Have them sit on the ground, legs stretched forward, and move the arms fast. When more confident, then move back to the feet.

Coaching tips

– Use the phrase "chin-hip" as they run. You want the hands to move in opposition from the chin down to the hip. You do not want the hands moving across the body.

– Even if they walk, that is OK; the focus here is on arm action.

NO ARMS

No Arms

 When running forward, if their torso/upper body moves from side to side a lot, this can signify weak abdominals.

Coaching tips

- Remember, make all these exercises playful and fun.
- Do the exercises with the child.

43

TREADMILL

Objective: To improve cardiovascular fitness and teach them how to use the treadmill properly.

 Don't be afraid to put on their favorite TV show to watch or music to listen to. We do it at the gym, so why shouldn't they?

How to

- Begin by having the child stand on the treadmill and then start the treadmill at around 1 mph. The child could be scared of it, so starting slowly is best. Be sure to fasten the emergency off-clip to their shirt or shorts.

- Gradually increase the speed as they become more accustomed to it. Faster is not always better, in terms of increasing fitness or weight loss.

- Make sure the child holds onto the handles bars if they feel uncomfortable.

- If there are many buttons on the machine, the child may want to explore or press them all. Cover up the ones that could cause problems...like the "Stop" button.

How many

- 1–20 minutes.

- Begin with walking, and slowly increase speed to a run. (This could take months.)

Coaching tips

- If they are having trouble staying on the treadmill, stand behind the child with your legs on the sides of the treadmill, to prevent them from trying to step off.

- Be the leader—have them watch you do it for five minutes and then have them try. *"First* Mom...*then* Johnny."

- Sometimes watching the tread move is more exciting then being on it, but encourage them to watch it while walking or running on it.

- If the child cannot run and only walks, gradually increase the incline of the treadmill. This will help to increase calorie burn and improve cardiovascular fitness.

Treadmill

44

CONE RUNNING

Objective: To improve cardiovascular fitness while working on motor planning and following directions.

 This same concept can be used to help the children learn to run the bases in baseball. Set up four cones in a diamond shape and try it!

How to

- Set up four cones at a distance that can be accomplished by the child. You can set up more or fewer cones if needed.

- Use a cadence familiar to the child to start the activity, such as, "Ready...set... go!"

- If the child is walking, do not push them to run. Let them figure out the pattern— that is half the challenge.

How to

- One to three sets or 1–5 laps.

Coaching tips

- Arrows on the ground can help to show the child which direction you want them to run in. Use sidewalk chalk, masking tape, or spray paint.

- Run with the child! Don't just talk the talk, walk the walk!

Cone Running

45

EXERCISE BIKE

Objective: To increase cardiovascular fitness while working to improve motor coordination for riding a bike.

 Children will burn less calories per workout when using a bike compared with a treadmill; however, a bike is safer to use.

How to

- As with all the exercises, demonstrate what you want the child to do.
- Adjust the seat so that when their knee is not fully extended when turning, there is a slight knee bend.
- Have the child sit on the bike and ask them to pedal. You may have to prompt them to move their legs.

How many

- 1–20 minutes.

Coaching tips

- If they are having trouble pressing down or not wanting to do it, try increasing the resistance; this may give them more sensory feedback.

Exercise Bike

46

TRAMPOLINE

Objective: To increase cardiovascular fitness, meet the child's sensory integration needs, and improve the fitness of the muscles in the ankles, knees, and hips.

 Have the child try to move their feet in a jumping jack pattern (apart–together) or shuffle them back and forth. Doing so will improve the strength of the ankles, knees, and hips while further challenging the brain!

How to

- Have the child stand on the trampoline, getting on one foot at a time.
- When the child is comfortable ask them to "jump" or show them a visual support card.

How many

- Perform one to five sets of 10–25 jumps.

Coaching tips

- If the child is not accustomed to this, holding their hands while jumping may help.
- It can also help if you are jumping, on the ground, as they are jumping.

Trampoline

REFERENCES

Bryan, L. and Gast, D. (2000) "Teaching on-task and on-schedule behaviors to high functioning children with autism via picture activity schedules." *Journal of Autism and Developmental Disorders 30*, 553–567.

Creera, D.J., Romberg, C., Saksida, L.M., van Praag, H., and Bussey, T.J. (2010) "Running enhances spatial pattern separation in mice." *PNAS 107*, 5, 2367–2372.

Dettmer, S., Simpson, R., Myles, B., and Ganz, J. (2000) "The use of visual supports to facilitate transitions of students with autism." *Focus on Autism and Other Developmental Disabilities 15*, 163–170.

Egan, A.M., Dreyer M.L., Odar, C.C., Beckwith, M., and Garrison, C.B. (2013) "Obesity in young children with autism spectrum disorders: Prevalence and associated factors." *Childhood Obesity 9*, 2, 125–131.

Erickson, K.I., Voss, M.W., Prakash, R.S., Basake, C., Szabo, A., Chaddock, L., Kim, J.S., Heo, S., Alves, H., White, S.M., Wojcicki, T.R., Mailey, E., Vieira, V.J., Martin, S.A., Pence, B.D., Woods, J.A., McAuley, E., and Kramer, A.F. (2011) "Exercise training increases size of hippocampus and improves memory." *PNAS 108*, 7.

Kendall, F., McCreary, E., and and Provance, P. (1993) *Muscles: Testing and Function with Posture and Pain.* 4th edn. Philadelphia, Pa: Lippincott Williams and Wilkins.

Krantz, P.J. and McClannahan, L.E. (1998) "Social interaction skills for children with autism: A script-fading procedure for beginning readers." *Journal of Applied Behavior Analysis 31*, 191–202.

MacDuff, G., Krantz, P., and McClannahan, L. (1993) "Teaching children with autism to use photographic activity schedules: Maintenance and generalization of complex response chains." *Journal of Applied Behavior Analysis 26*, 89–97.

Mahoney, G. and Perales, F. (2005) "Relationship-focused early intervention with children with pervasive developmental disorders and other disabilities: A comparative study." *Journal of Developmental and Behavioral Pediatrics 26*, 2, 77–85.

Massey, G. and Wheeler, J. (2000) "Acquisition and generalization of activity schedules and their effects on task engagement in a young child with autism in an inclusive preschool classroom." *Education and Training in Mental Retardation and Developmental Disabilities 35*, 326–335.

McCleery, J.P., Elliott, N.A., Sampanis, D.S., and Stepanidou, C.A. (2013) "Motor development and motor resonance difficulties in autism: relevance to early intervention for language and communication skills." Journal of Autism and Developmental Disorder. Doi: 10.3389/fnint.2013.00030.

Morrison, R., Sainato, D., Benchaaban, D., and Endo, S. (2002) "Increasing play skills of children with autism using activity schedules and correspondence training." *Journal of Early Intervention 25*, 58–72.

Nieman, D.C. (1999) *Exercise Testing and Prescription: A Health-Related Approach*. 4th edn. Mountain View, CA: Mayfield.

O'Connor, J.H., French, R., and Henderson, H. (2000) "Use of physical activity to improve behaviour of children with autism." *Palestra 16*, 3, 5.

Rosenthal-Malek, A. and Mitchell, S. (1997) "Brief report: The effects of exercise on the self-stimulating behaviors and positive responding of adolescents with autism." *Journal of Autism and Developmental Disorders 27*, 2, 193–202.

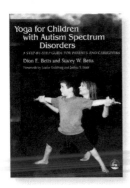

Yoga for Children with Autism Spectrum Disorders

A Step-by-Step Guide for Parents and Caregivers

Dion E. Betts and Stacey W. Betts

Foreword by Louise Goldberg and Joshua S. Betts

Paperback: £12.99/$19.95

ISBN: 978 1 84310 817 7

104 pages

Having successfully used yoga to combat the stress of their own busy lives, Dion and Stacey Betts discovered its potential for their son Joshua, who has Asperger Syndrome.

This fully-illustrated book combines the authors' professional expertise with their experience of parenting, offering a range of gentle and fun yoga positions and breathing techniques that are effective in dealing with the increased levels of anxiety, disorientation and tactile sensitivity often found in children with autism spectrum disorders (ASDs).

The authors give step-by-step descriptions of warming-up, strengthening, calming, and tension-releasing exercises that are suitable for reducing coping mechanisms, such as hand-flapping, and increasing muscle tone, muscle strength and body awareness. They also offer a range of short and long sequences that can be tailored to fit the needs of the individual child.

Yoga for Children with Autism Spectrum Disorders is ideal for parents and caregivers who want to use simple yoga techniques to help children with ASDs overcome some of the symptoms of the disorder.

Contents: Preface. A note on this book. Foreword by Louise Goldberg, Registered Yoga Teacher. Foreword by Joshua S. Betts. Introduction. 1: How to Use This Guide. Sequence of yoga poses. Modifications of poses and sessions. Demonstrate poses to your child. Ensure that your child is comfortable. A note on breathing. Motivating children with Autism Spectrum Disorders to practice yoga. 2: The Yoga Sequence for Children with Autism Spectrum Disorders. Warm-up Poses. Sitting Pose. Cat Pose. Shoulder Opener Pose. Neck Rolls. Mountain Pose. Spinal Rolls. Chair Pose. Strengthening Poses. Triangle Pose. Side Angle Pose. Downward Dog Pose. Warrior I Pose. Warrior II Pose. Standing Forward Bend Pose (A and B). Tree Pose. Release of Tension Poses. Sphinx Pose. Boat Pose. Bridge Pose. Calming Poses. Sitting Forward Bend Pose. Spread Leg Forward Bend Pose. Head-to-Knee Pose. Butterfly Pose. Reclining Butterfly Pose. Seated Spinal Twist Pose. Easy Spinal Twist Pose. Child's Pose. Corpse Pose. 3: Yogic Breathing. Ujjayi Breathing. Skull Shining Breath. Curled Tongue Breath. Lion Breath. Alternate Nostril Breathing. 4: Shorter Yoga Sequences. Short sequence 1. Short sequence 2. References

Dion E. Betts, Ed.D., is Superintendent of Schools, Boyertown Area School District, USA.

Stacey W. Betts is an attorney and assists families with children with disabilities. Dion E. Betts, Ed.D., is Assistant to the Superintendent for Instructional Support at South Western School District in Hanover, PA. Dion and Stacey are the authors of Yoga for Children with Autism Spectrum Disorders, and Dion is co-author of Homespun Remedies: Strategies in the Home and Community for Children with Autism Spectrum and Other Disorders, both published by Jessica Kingsley Publishers. Stacey and Dion live in Lancaster, PA with their five children, one of whom has AS.

Yoga Therapy for Every Special Child
Meeting Needs in a Natural Setting
Nancy Williams
Illustrated by Leslie White
Published by Singing Dragon
Paperback: £12.99/$19.95
ISBN: 978 1 84819 027 6
208 pages

Yoga therapy is gaining rapid recognition as a form of treatment that can improve the physical and mental wellbeing of children with a variety of complex needs. This book contains a specially-designed yoga program for use with children of all abilities, and provides both parents and professionals with the knowledge they need to carry out the therapy themselves.

The program consists of a series of postures, each of which is explained and accompanied by an illustration. The postures are designed to help children understand and use their bodies, and work towards positive changes such as realigning the spine, encouraging eye-contact, and promoting calm and steady breathing. Consideration is given to creating the right setting for carrying out the therapy, assessing an individual child's particular needs, and making the sessions fun using games and props. Sections on yoga therapy for specific conditions such as autistic spectrum disorder, Down syndrome, and cerebral palsy are included, and the book concludes with child and parent reports on how the program has worked for them, and a list of useful contacts and resources.

This practical book is a must for parents, teachers, therapists and other professionals, and anybody else who wants to help a child to develop through enjoyable and therapeutic yoga sessions.

Contents: Dedication. Acknowledgements. Preface. 1. Introduction. Normal Development. Developmental Challenges. Similarities of Yoga and Neuro-developmental Therapy (NDT). Yoga Meets Therapy Goals. 2. The Benefits of Yoga. The Breath. Body Awareness. Motor Planning. Spirit of Communication. Behavioural Self-regulation. Social Skills. Universal Awareness. Multidisciplinary. Sensory Integration. Natural Setting. Multidimensional Approach. Healthy Body. Restorative. Sleep Patterns. Skill Set. Energetic Alignment. 3. Getting Ready. Creating a Space. When, How Often, and for How Long? Assessment by Observation. Introducing the Setting. Paradigm for Success. 4. The Yoga Program. Namasté. Breath Work. Tibetan Bells. Mudra and Mantras. Postures. Savasana with Guided Imagery. Closing Mudra and Mantra. 5. Yoga and the Energy Body. The Root Chakra - Stability. The Navel Chakra - Relationship and Creativity. The Solar Plexus Chakra - Self-esteem. The Heart Chakra - Love and Compassion. The Throat Chakra - Communication. The Brow Chakra - Divine Vision. The Crown Chakra - Spiritual Connection. 6. Yoga Games. Games to Build Strength. Mudra and Mantra Games. Games to Build Confidence. Games Using Props and Toys. Breathing Games. Games to develop Imagination. 7. Yoga for Specific Conditions. Precautions. Attention Deficit/Hyperactivity Disorder. Autism Spectrum Disorder. Cancer. Cerebral Palsy. Compromised Respiration. Developmental Delay. Down Syndrome. Emotional Sensitivity. Fluency Disorder. Hemiparesis. High Tone. Language Delay and/or Disorder. Low Tone. Post Traumatic Stress Disorder. Sensory Integration Disorder. Social Communication Delay. Scoliosis. 8. The Response. Yogis and Parents. References. Resources. Glossary. Index.

Nancy Williams has been a yoga therapist for 9 years. During this time, she has worked with children with a wide range of special needs, including Autism Spectrum disorders, cerebral palsy, sensory integration disorder and Down's syndrome. Nancy also works as a pediatric Speech Pathologist, and is a certified Neuro Developmental Treatment Therapist, Zero Balancing practitioner, Yoga instructor and Reiki Master Teacher. Nancy owns Therapeutic Bodyworks, a studio in Tucson, Arizona where she teaches yoga therapy classes to individual and small groups of children. Nancy also offers consultations and conducts training workshops.

Everyday Activities to Help Your Young Child with Autism Live Life to the Full
Simple Exercises to Boost Functional Skills, Sensory Processing, Coordination and Self-Care
Debra S. Jacobs and Dion E. Betts
Foreword by Carol A. Just
Paperback: £14.99/$19.95
ISBN: 978 1 84905 238 2
144 pages

Does your child struggle with brushing their teeth? Is it difficult to get them dressed and undressed each day? Do they struggle to understand their body's relationship to the world?

This book is brimming with simple ideas, activities and exercises to address these daily challenges that young children with autism face. Easy to carry out and to fit into your routines, they will help improve a child's sense of body awareness, coordination and motor skills, and address key tasks such as eating meals and healthy sleep. There are also ideas for tackling social challenges, including playing with friends, going on holiday and staying calm at school. The final chapter of the book explains the different support professionals parents of a child with autism are likely to encounter and how each can help their child.

This jargon-free book shows how occupational therapy techniques can be used to help your young child with autism to live life to the full, and will be an essential tool for parents and carers.

Contents: Acknowledgements. A Note About This Book. Foreword by Carol A. Just. Introduction. 1. Body Awareness. 2. Increasing Coordination. 3. Fine Motor Skills. 4. Understanding the World Through the Senses. 5. Daily Living Skills. 6. Activities in the Home, School and Community. 7. Calming Techniques. 8. Building Capacity: Optimizing Care and Treatment.

Debra S. Jacobs is an occupational therapist in private practice and also at Tucson Unified School District, USA.

Dion E. Betts, Ed.D., is Superintendent of Schools, Boyertown Area School District, USA.